HITTING HOME

WITH FUNDAMENTAL PURPOSE AND INTENT.

FOR BASEBALL AND SOFTBALL HITTERS

FOREWORD BY JAKE BOSS
BOBBY F. HUMPHREY

AuthorHouse™
1663 Liberty Drive
Bloomington, IN 47403
www.authorhouse.com
Phone: 1 (800) 839-8640

This book is printed on acid-free paper.

Interior Image Credit: James Beeler

ISBN: 978-1-7283-2078-6 (sc)
ISBN: 978-1-7283-2079-3 (e)

Print information available on the last page.

Published by AuthorHouse   07/30/2019

TABLE OF CONTENTS

FOREWORD

By Jake Boss,
Michigan State University
Head Baseball Coach

With an abundance of resources, especially via social media, hitting "instruction" is right in the palm of everyone's hands. The topic of hitting can be found around every corner, by every self-labeled guru, easily accessible by every coach, parent, and player, all with one click of a button. The amount of instruction out there has never been higher, from social media to private instructors. Consequently, the amount of *misinformation* has also never been higher, and it can be difficult to navigate the good and the bad.

As Coach Humphrey discusses, all good coaches utilize and share information in a solid network of teaching and learning, and this book and its instructional focus is a fantastic piece of the puzzle that fits well, especially intended for youth through high school coaches.

With his in-depth experience and collaboration with high-level coaches, Coach Humphrey has put together a framework that prioritizes the most critical, need-to-know elements of hitting that is precise and simplified, including effective hitting instruction, individual development, and practice planning. In an era of over-coaching, this book serves as a definitive tool to be used as immediate implementation with individuals and teams.

From my playing days at Alma College, through coaching at the NCAA Division 1 level, I have seen many attempted changes and an over use of jargon and phrases, adjustments in the teachings of basic ideas, and searches for the proper twists and turns to allow for players to hit more efficiently. Ultimately, hitting has changed very little over time, despite the latest buzz words, and Coach Humphrey reminds us of this. Develop a plan, be organized, and stay away from extremes. Ultimately, when players get to the college level, we want kids to be able to hit with consistency and compete in all situations and hitting counts.

With every quality soundbite and piece of information out there, resources are to be utilized with an ultimate goal – to help young people succeed. Coaches will always look for ways to get ahead, gain an edge, and create new advances for hitting.

Coach Humphrey keeps it simple and relevant to all, in a refreshing, applicable look at developing hitters. Rather than overload with the intricacies of swing analysis, he offers a must-have resource for baseball and softball parents, players, and especially coaches.

ACKNOWLEDGEMENT

During the summer prior to my senior year at Spring Arbor University, a group of high school friends – some playing college, some not – decided to get together to create our own summer team – an independent team of sorts. My most memorable at-bat came during the final game that summer, playing a double header against a team from Sault St. Marie, Canada.

My dad was our coach that summer, and I was in the batters' box for what would surely be the last time I played with Dad as my head coach. Half choked up, Mom approached me from the stands.

"Hit a homerun for your dad," Mom said with tears in her eyes.

Hitting a homerun on command is not necessarily an easy feat, and I was a bit taken aback. I was excited and well aware that I would never play another game with Dad at third base. But a homerun!? Come on, Mom! As we are often reminded, one should always listen to Mom. I did. On the first pitch, I got a belt high fastball and sent it to dead center field. That hand shake will forever be my favorite moment in my athletic career, playing or coaching.

While playing video games was not exactly an enticing activity, I also give special thanks to my brother, John Sczykutowicz for making sure I was outside much more than inside. We had many nights of wiffle ball!

I am forever grateful for the incredible blessings I have had as my leaders. My dad. Coach John Gerhardt. Coach Ian Hearn and Coach Brad Balentine. And of course my coaches at Spring Arbor, Hank Burbridge and Sam Rigglemen, both ABCA and NAIA Hall of Fame coaches.

All coaches are lifelong learners of not only the game, but the leadership aspects that include a strong moral compass, communication with young people, and team building. I thank those coaches for the support and shared knowledge over the years, and especially during the writing of this book. All coaches have learned from others, and the willingness to share and generate ideas exemplifies an ambassador role for baseball and softball, with one primary goal – to help young people succeed.

Special thanks to my many fifth grade students, whose dreams are still undoubted, encouraged, and very real.

Finally, thanks to my wife, Kendra, for encouraging my passions.

PREFACE

In my experience as a player, coach and scout, there are two absolutes on the instructional side of baseball and softball: **Catching** is easily the most under-coached aspect of the game, and **hitting** is easily the most over-coached aspect of the game

Unfortunately, hitting is also the most egotistical area of both softball and baseball. Everyone is an expert, regardless of experience, and everyone's opinion is right. What I have found to be most often true with people that get red-faced with their know-it-all self-proclamation is that they run with something they heard or saw once. They saw one coach say it. They heard it on TV. They push one particular concept without understanding big-picture ideals. Good coaches are always learning and always improving themselves for the betterment of young people. Through that comes a constant, continual learning curve, open to new ideas and feedback. When the American Baseball Coaches' Association (ABCA) has conventions with over 5,000 coaches, some of which are the very best on globe, they are there to network, share ideas, and above all else, learn from others.

This book is not intended to target a particular player, because that is not how hitting works. Instead, it is a guide for coaches to implement effective teachings through basic principles, organized plans, and deeper understanding of both individualistic and team hitting. My hope in writing this book is that it sheds light on the priorities of hitting, misconceptions, and it helps to build a foundation of team and individual development. This book has been designed as a use now resource – an easy read to begin developing hitters more efficiently. Fundamental implementation can begin immediately.

If anything, above all, I want players and coaches to come away with these basic principles:

- **All hitters are different**
- **A good swing is a good swing, baseball or softball**
- **Hitting improvement takes time**
- **Simplify mechanics**
- **Approach is as important as swing mechanics**
- **Drills must have purpose**
- **Gimmicks should be avoided**
- **Team practice is to be organized with as much movement as possible**

There are a lot of strong hitting coaches out there and I encourage coaches to utilize all resources. Coaches, like their players, should embrace a lifelong learning posture. With a simplified, specific breakdown of what I believe to be the most important areas of hitter development, this book should provide enough detail and planning to allow all coaches to improve self and their team.

Simplify

As an Associate Scout, I have seen thousands of hitters during my career. I have seen hundreds of stances, and many strengths and weaknesses of MLB-bound hitters. I have broken down film with scouting personnel on dozens of hitters. Players that stand tall and players that are more crouched. Players that get more linear, and others that are more rotational. Open stances and closed stances. Coil. Leg kick.

Coach what works for the individual!

The one conclusion all can draw: you can watch any hitter on the planet in slow motion and find flaws from swing-to-swing. The final thing we look for as scouts and as coaches is *production*.

A hitter with a less than perfect swing can still hit. A number of coaches obsess over perfecting that swing to make a baseball card. Don't! Even top, elite hitters have breakdowns in their swing from time to time, and flaws don't necessarily equate to poor hitting. I have watched high-round draft picks with minor flaws, noticeable during evaluations, go on to reach the MLB level. Obviously adjustments for those hitters continued after college, into the Minor Leagues, and will continue for the duration of their career. But it's about production, not a model swing.

> *"Coaches need to unlock the individual athlete. Too much of a mechanical focus devalues the athlete's ability. When you talk mechanics too much you're putting hitter's in a tough situation by creating too many focuses that take away from the main focus of hitting the ball hard."*
>
> *Eddie Smith – Hitting Coach,* Louisiana State University

Never have I said that the mechanics of a swing were unimportant. But hitting is over-coached and over-analyzed. I appreciate sciences and the use of technology, but we must also understand that that each hitter is different, and use of such technologies must be accompanied by deep understanding of human movement and general hitting.

Pete Rose put it simply: "See the ball, hit the ball."

We know that hitting isn't quite that easy. What coaches should be mindful of is balance in philosophies and methods. Fix what is necessary – flaws that are prohibiting the player to be successful at the plate, but don't attempt to create robotic hitters.

Mechanics should be seen as a ground-up approach.

As coaches analyze swings, often if there is an issue it's immediate for some to look at the start of the bat, when in fact the feet may begin the issue, causing a domino effect. The swing begins with balance and timing. For example, if a player continues to hit weak pop ups, it's not necessarily that the bat bath is the core of the problem. It could be that the player is lunging, over-striding, and generally does not have good timing, beginning with their feet. Some bad swings also begin with having a poor approach, because swinging at bad pitches also alters the swing. Look to simplify first.

> *"You do whatever it takes to consistently get the barrel to the ball. Then you perfect it. Be an expert with your bat path and what your body does."*
> *Jim Thompson – Area Supervisor,* New York Mets

Softball and baseball swings are no different.

In an effort to grow as a softball coach, I made connections with people throughout the country and discussed hitting. I chose former college and professional players and coaches, and from those coaches that have won at the very pinnacle of college softball, the feedback was always the same – there is no difference, and a good swing is a good swing. The only thing I can gather from those that argue against it is that they're forming a "versus" mentality between the two sports, instead of an acknowledgement that you're doing the same thing. There are some subtle differences in everyone's swing, but if we are focusing on the priority areas of hitting, there is absolutely no difference – balance, bat path, and timing, in addition to approach, pitch recognition, and plate coverage. Drills are universally the same, so how we can say the swing is different? When Jennie Finch and her instructors visited the Shenandoah Valley, I was there, eager to learn from some of the best. The hitting instruction was no different than I had seen at any baseball camp around the country.

> *"There is no difference. At the end of the day there are different styles of hitting, but the elite are all similar within the actual swing. The swing is only one aspect to actual hitting, and approaches are different in levels, along with teaching individual adjustments needed. The bottom line is an elite swing is an elite swing, whether it's baseball or softball."*
> *Keith Parr – Head Softball Coach,* Christopher Newport University

Years ago, there was a particular difference for some, which limited girls' ability. Outdated instruction had softball players develop a flattened swing, while also limiting power. Furthermore, some emphasized hitting the top of the ball, with the idea being to hit hard ground balls. This sets limitations, when in truth, all good hitters can drive the ball with power and authority.

Another "difference" some people attempt to push is the ability to hit the rise ball. What changes in the swing? You're still swinging to get on plane, and hitting mechanics don't change mid-pitch, when you have less than one half of a second to adjust.

> *"A good swing is a good swing. The ability to hit through a long zone and make adjustments*
> *to speed, location, and movement must be accomplished in either baseball or softball."*
> *Mike Candrea – Head Softball Coach,* University of Arizona

Every aspect of this book is to be utilized on both the softball and baseball fields. There is no difference.

Stance:

Look at some baseball cards. Google your favorite players of every generation. You're going to find dozens of different stances, some of which are completely unorthodox, such as Mickey Tettleton, Julio Franco, and Craig Counsel. From upright hitters like Ken Griffey Junior, to slightly athletic positions like Alex Rodriguez and Mike Trout, to lower stances like Jeff Bagwell, they all have the same thing in common at the point of contact – balance.

When working with especially young players, I oftentimes see a heavy backside lean. You may see MLB-level players on TV with various, funky stances, but balance is supremely important, and while it may appear awkward, all of those guys will have weight distribution, especially at the end of their load, and at the point of contact. Be athletic.

I would not take the approach that players must stand the same, but their own stance *is* critically important:

- Is there balance?
- Does their stance allow for minimal head movement?
- How much does the bat have to move into an adequate load – or launch – position from the stance?
- Does the stance allow their body to remain mobile and loose, from the first movement of the load, through the point of contact?
- Are the hitter's hands at or above the top of the strike zone, especially when beginning the load?

How do you "fix" a stance? This is where it gets tricky, because it depends entirely on the player. You can consider the previous questions, and adjustments could include widening of feet, quieting down the bat, or closing and opening of the feet, among others.

General Stance – a Guide:

- Feet shoulder-width apart, with balanced weight
- Slight flex in the knees to be athletic
- Hands above the top of the K zone

This is not an absolute, but if I'm working with young players, or there is a clear flaw in their ability to hit, the first area I look is the stance. Why is a player not able to hit the ball effectively in all zones? It may begin before their load even begins.

Load:

There should be some negative movement, in the form of a load. The load is dependent upon the hitter. The point of the load is to create body separation, looseness of the swing, bat speed, and a good angle in which the bat can come through the zone. When I scout during BP, or before I begin evaluations as a coach and/or hitting instructor, the load is one of the first mechanics I look at. For players that struggle with understanding a load, it can be simplified to minimal movement – the bottom hand pushes the bat back slightly.

Years ago during a showcase in Miami, I had the opportunity to visit the late Paul Casanova and his hitting shrine – a covered hitting area in his backyard. He worked with Miami-area hitters ranging from youth levels, through prominent MLB All-Stars. As you walked in, the first thing you noticed were the pictures – all over the place. Every picture, from Willie Mayes to current MLB stars scattered the walls and were hanging overhead. All of them were of each batter in their load, and that was exactly the point. Of course, all loads have some differences, but Casanova emphasized the 45 degree angle, and was able to do so by showing many of Major League Baseball's greatest stars, past and present. From that angle, you can successfully get on plane, from the launch position, to a pitched ball. Below we see different loads within the 45-degree angle range – with some differences. Search further loads by a basic internet search to see more, including some of your favorite players.

Proper Loading Basics:

- The bat should not "wrap" around the hitter's head, flattened out, with the top of the barrel directly behind the hitter's *neck*. This creates an unnecessarily long bat path to the ball. The above softball hitter is *not* wrapping.
- Coaches often use the term "arm bar", which means that the bottom arm of the hitter straightens, and locks at the backside of the load – the end of the load. Locking the bat creates stiffness in the swing, which reduces bat speed and the ability to cover all parts of the plate. Don't confuse the term "arm bar" with someone that may have a more exaggerated load, however. When the load stops its movement and locks at the backside, that's when it creates mechanical issues.
- The bat head should be at *roughly* a 45 degree angle. Too flat will cause bat drag, prohibiting the ability to hit inside pitches. If the bat head is straight up, it essentially ruins the swing, causing a hard, back shoulder drop, and an exaggerated hitch because the top hand will lead.

Swing:

Get even. Purposeful contact.

Breaking down a young player's swing is where I start to cringe, even through the college level. The more coaches try to perfect a swing, the more confusing it can be for a young person to hit! Fix what's broken, and do so through a progression of proper drills.

Having a solid mechanical swing is an important part of the hitting process, but coaches can cause significantly more harm than good by telling a hitter to focus on various mechanical components.

The very basics in swing mechanics are:

- Get on the same plane as the ball. The bat path should "get even" to the pitch location. This is what creates the "launch angle," which has really never changed over time.
- Be sure the shoulders remain closed on the swing, at the point of contact. We hear the term "flying open." That is when the shoulders open along with the core, which takes away the ability to cover the plate.
- Two jargon words, "linear" and "rotational," are exactly that – jargon words. Most good swings are both linear – forward movement, and rotational – using the core and hips to create torque within the swing. Some players may have *more* linear movement, or *more* rotational movement.
- Be on time – the front foot comes down to initiate the swing. The weight transfer to the front side should be balanced. A heavy front side causes lunging. Stride to balance, not to the ball.

- The hands, on the path of the ball, should remain "inside of the ball." The purpose here is to keep from casting the hands, which wrap around the outside of the ball. Staying inside the ball allows for the bat to come through the zone with a short, compact swing that allows the barrel to stay in the zone through the swing.
- Upon contact, the back foot may move forward slightly, or it may remain in position. This depends on the individual. Some players' back foot remains and pivots, others come forward slightly. If anything, stay away from the term "squashing the bug" because it's faulty instruction.
- The path of the bat does not change based on inside/outside swings with the exception of staying on plane. We do not teach hitters to step toward outside pitches. Instead, the points of contact change – out front for an inside pitch, and deeper in the zone for an outside pitch. The contact point for an outside pitch is roughly even with the hitter's *front* leg, and there are slight differences in shoulder position and back posture. I see drills showing the hitter taking outside pitches off of their back leg, and even deeper. This is a foul ball! The location of the contact point for outside pitches depends on where the hitter sets up, as well as the hitter's stride.

The Bottom Line:

A coach pointing out particular flaws is not necessarily a bad thing, but it's all in *how* we approach those flaws. If a player is hitting effectively, we cannot be so quick to jump in and fix something! The coach should *speak after the batting practice reps* and offer some drill work to modify the swing, with detailed rationalization. Players must *understand in order to apply.*

It's at this point where a productive hitter can be negatively impacted by basically thinking too much. There is a very fine line between proper mechanical feedback and overanalyzing. At the point of overanalyzing, a hitter could take big steps back and find themselves in a miserable hitting slump. **To maximize feedback, it should begin with a progression of drills, not only verbal feedback.**

Before fixing everything, look big picture and see the player as an individual. I was once at a college softball practice and stood back while watching a young lady take swings off the tee. After about five swings she turned around and asked me what she could work on. To no fault of this young lady, she was looking for feedback. As I was not an official coach with this program, this was the first time I saw the player with a bat in her hand. I explained to her that for me to give mechanical feedback of her swing would be poor coaching on my part and completely counterproductive. I need to see much more than five swings to give proper feedback! The point is, we often rush to fix without actually knowing if a problem even exists. It would be like taking a car to the shop and having them change your tires for an engine problem without actually doing a diagnostic. In this girl's case, I was looking more at the efficiency of the drill, not her swing – drills with a purpose.

While at Spring Arbor, Coach Hank Burbridge used to always tell us that if we could hit effectively with the bat in our teeth, he wasn't touching our swing. I appreciated this greatly, and it made it much more impactful when he did actually make adjustments. Because he did not attempt to perfect any of us, we took feedback more seriously. The feedback was typically minimal and something we could implement immediately.

> "Sometimes we see only one swing instead of the overall body of work. Hitting is taught over time, and some want instant feedback, which isn't realistic."
> Bill Cilento – Associate Head Baseball Coach, Wake Forest University

Major League Baseball Emulation:

I have always said that young players do not watch the game enough at the highest levels. This includes both baseball and softball players. Watching games and sport-specific shows on TV are invaluable, and I encourage players and coaches to take note and learn the game – the whole game. There is always information that can be used to improve coaches and players alike. That said, we also have to draw a line in our understanding that not everything you see on TV is applicable to younger players, especially youth through varsity-aged kids. Using something an MLB player is doing for a 14-year-old may be unwise; it's up to the coach to educate himself/herself and understand his or her players. A drill, approach, or mechanical adjustment that works for the world's most elite players may not for a 14-year-old. When in doubt, drop the jargon and catch words, and focus on the basics. You can never go wrong with the basics!

> "Physicality at the MLB level is so different. You can't always apply the same things with youth levels. Major League players are always making adjustments to work through their swing. I see players on the back end of their careers that are still making adjusments."
> Keith Werman – Development Coordinator, San Diego Padres

Technology Feedback:

Technological advances are going to continue, and they're a fantastic tool. We have the ability to track a player's swing, exit velocity, and launch angle. We can hit indoors and have immediate feedback on all analytics, as well as how far the ball would have traveled. The knowledge and feedback we have at our fingertips is indisputably better for sports.

The powerful use of technology comes in the after – how is it put to use? What are we doing after swing analysis? What is the next step? Before looking at flaws, coaches should look for strengths in a swing to be built upon, because if we are only focused on the negative feedback of technology, the impact on players can have an adverse effect. Remember that not every swing will always be the same, so pointing out one swing's flaws is often unnecessary. Instead, look at a series of swings, and if in fact there is a clear flaw, address it through proper drill work.

While watching a young man hit at a facility, I witnessed the adverse effects of immediate replay. The push was entirely mechanical, and after each short round of swings, the instructor and young man evaluated every robotic step of the swing together. The swing "improved" and the praise was clear, but the contact of the ball decreased. But he looked good.

Use technology with purpose and a plan. A player that understands the how and the why can effectively make adjustments. Proper use of technology can be eye opening, but it must be partnered with approach and adequate drill work.

Social Media Experts – Beware!

Imagine if a college coach watched one slow-motion video of a prospect and made their determination. What if scouts made draft determinations after seeing one open-side view of a hitter? There is no fault for a parent to want feedback, but I see social media posts of one swing that gets hundreds of comments on what they're doing incorrectly. Stay away from that! Also, more times than not, what parents are really looking for on social media is flattering feedback for the ego, not true feedback about an athletic ability. But parents have to consider the sources of feedback, which include people that never touched a field, but feel necessary to insert their oftentimes aggressive, "measuring stick" knowledge (I know more than you!), or lack thereof.

Keep your kids' swings, throws, and other athletic evaluations off open social media pages. Instead, use people you trust. Send video to a coach that you know, with good credentials. Talk to that hitting instructor you're probably seeing.

Being on Time. By Derrick May, Former MLB Player and Hitting Coach:

"Being on time is probably the single most important – and biggest issue – many hitters face when trying to hit a baseball or softball. Timing issues will break down any hitter's swing (in my opinion) 90% of the time.

In the confrontation between the hitter and the pitcher...pitchers don't play fair. And this is why hitting is hard. Pitchers consistently try to disrupt the timing and balance of hitters by using effective velocity, tunneling, movement, and off speed.

What is being on time? For many it's about getting back (hands, backside, or both depending on how you hit) early enough to get the barrel out in front or to the pitch location on time and getting the foot down at the right time.

*When do you start to get ready? This usually depends on the individual. Some hitters will start when they see the pitcher's backside, some when they see the pitcher break his hands and some will start a little later depending on what pre-swing movements they have. Being in a good position is crucial to seeing and hitting the ball. **Walks are byproducts of being ready to hit and so is driving the baseball.***

After the pitch is released a hitter's timing has just begun. Being back early enough will help hitters see the ball. Good hitters work off the fastball and are ready to hit it.

What does this mean? A hitter will be ready for a fastball and adjust to off speed. It is very hard to look for off speed and still hit a good fastball. Good hitters know this. That's why understanding timing is important. Timing is not only being back early enough. It also has to do with the stride.

The stride is what pitchers look to disrupt – things like getting a hitter out in front or getting his foot down too early or too late, and speeding him up and slowing him down. This is all timing and pitchers understand this very well.

The stride plays a huge part because hitters look for consistent, repeatable mechanics which includes the stride length. A hitter will spend hours trying to make his or her swing become automatic and repeatable. Stride length is a big part of that.

When the stride is disrupted, so is timing. One technique used is to get the foot down early. But too early will disrupt momentum, causing the hitter to stop and restart again. The stride must be fluid and organic, not forced. Do you think about putting your foot down when you walk?

When making a positive move towards the pitcher as the pitch is released, the pitch will dictate the stride length. When executed properly, a stride to a fastball will be at normal stride length and the stride to an off speed pitch may be slightly longer depending on how well a hitter can wait or what they are expecting.

Good hitters are able to make adjustments from pitch to pitch and understand who they are facing."

APPROACH

Prepared and On Time

Ask a high school player. Even ask a college player. "What is your hitter's count approach?" The answers will range from deer-in-headlights, to a ramble that may make some sense, and if they really have an understanding of what they're doing at the plate, a definitive response for varying situations. If there is any section of this book to tune into the most, this is it. Hitters must have an approach. A perfect swing without an approach is…a perfect swing. Nothing more.

In simplest terms, having an approach means understanding your strengths and weaknesses at the plate, as well as understanding the differences in a hitter's count and hitting with two strikes. Coaches often say, "Look for your pitch," and that is essentially having an approach. But we can be more definitive and clear in our mental approach. Outside of the professional ranks and top-tier collegiate levels, most hitters should have a good enough approach and plate discipline to be aggressive with less than two strikes, ***rarely being fooled.***

Good hitters are such because they have an excellent approach to go along with good physical tools. Teach hitters to focus on their zone (example follows) with less than two strikes, reading the ball immediately out of the pitcher's hand to prepare for an aggressive swing only within their red zone.

Hitters must consider their "red zones", or "hot zones" – the part of the strike zone they consider to be their greatest strength. Players can consider what they may see on TV or in video games. Within a strike zone, red colored squares indicate the hitter's primary "hot zone."

Hitter's Count Approach:

Generally speaking, I consider most at-bats with less than two strikes to be a "hitter's count." To have an approach is to **have a pre-pitch preparedness**; you're looking for one pitch within your red zone. That zone does not have to be baseball/softball-sized, however. Below is a chart demonstrating where a hitter may be looking in pitch counts with less than two strikes.

Sample "Hot Zone" Hitting Chart – Mine Personally

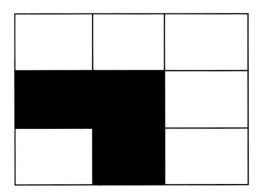

Ideally, any hitter that steps to the plate against any pitching is looking for a pitch to swing at with aggression. Hitters should **rarely be fooled in hitters' count situations.** When at the plate, the hitter is zeroed in on one relative location (above example) and when the pitch is within that zone, an aggressive "BP" swing is taken. Swinging at pitches out of the zone or being fooled by slow breaking balls demonstrates a lack of approach and plate discipline. During games, I often use the phrase "BP swing only," which tells my hitter that they are sitting on a pitch – usually a fastball – within his or her red zone. Good hitters make pitchers pay for their mistakes by way of attacking their red zone. Set. Load. Timing. React and attack in *your zone*.

Have you ever had a hitter take a weak swing, and gesture or vocalize, "Ugh" in a hitter's count? Approach. They were not prepared on that pitch. Lock in and make pitchers pay for their mistakes!

"Your 'A' swing is the function of pitch selection."
Jim Thompson – Area Supervisor, New York Mets

"Yes, yes, no."
Never be late on a pitch with less than two strikes. ***It's a pre-pitch, prepared mentality.*** Coaches oftentimes use the phrase, "Yes, yes, no." You're swinging at your hot zone until you're not; you're looking for a BP pitch until it's not in your zone.

"Sometimes hitters come back from an at-bat and want immediate feedback. The majority of the time it has nothing to do with mechanics; it is instead pitch selection."
Joe Abraham – Head Softball Coach, University of Toledo

Two Strike Approach:

Some players may want to choke up on the bat a bit. Some get closer, or crowd the plate. Some may get into a bit lower crouch.

During one scouting evaluation a young man ended an at-bat with a shallow fly ball to the outfield. He demonstrated an exceptional two-strike approach, however. His swing mechanics and aggressiveness with the bat did not change. During the course of the at-bat, he hit one off the fence, just foul to the opposite field, and also protected the inner half of the plate with a hard pull for another foul. With the same mechanics and swing path, the batter fouled off at least one fastball, change up, and breaking ball. While the at-bat was not successful, the demonstration of this approach was impressive. He didn't simply "throw the hands" to make weak contact. His zone expanded and he covered it very well. **This needs to be practiced! Cover all parts of the plate and learn to adjust**. Making this point to teams through discussion is not good enough; you must **practice this approach**.

As hitters get to the level when off-speed pitches become adequate, the approach should almost always be to look fastball and adjust to off-speed. At advanced levels – college and beyond – pitcher scouting reports may allow for a hitter to look for a breaking ball. Otherwise, anytime a good catcher or coach hears an opposing player say, "Watch for the curve," it's an easy choice for a fastball up and in on the hitter. Looking off-speed – in most situations – makes the hitter incredibly vulnerable.

An appropriate two-strike approach is to first look fastball on the outer half, making necessary adjustments as needed. To look outer half is to also support balance and swing path if and when an off-speed pitch is thrown. With good balance (not lunging) a hitter can adequately adjust their swing to hit the off-speed pitch. Turning on an inside fastball is a mere reaction in this situation. Sitting fastball inside in an 0-2 count makes it difficult to hit hard stuff on the outside part of the plate.

From the 3B box, I often give very simple direction: "Look fastball and adjust." This is a reminder that the player is looking for something straight, and will adjust to a breaking ball. This is especially important as velocities begin to increase.

First Pitch Strike:

What are pitchers taught? Generally speaking, both softball and baseball pitchers are taught to get ahead early. They do so to put further pressure on the hitter by expanding their zone. To work ahead, pitchers are taught to pound the strike zone, right? Once they're ahead they can pitch near the black, or off of the plate. Some coaches may have different philosophies, but this is typically true.

Fine. Why would we tell hitters to see a strike – **if a general rule on the team** – if we are also telling the pitchers to get ahead by pounding the strike zone? This doesn't make sense. The data is overwhelmingly in favor of attacking the ball, *if in your zone*, with no strikes. Some coaches have this as a team guideline, top through bottom, regardless of what is happening in the game, and it's completely unsupported by data.

Hit the ball! This approach should have little difference compared to a 2-0 count. Prepare. Attack your red zone.

As baseball and softball has many scenarios and situations, taking until getting a strike can be the most reasonable thinking, depending on circumstances, but *absolutely not as a team approach*, as a rule to be followed always. A lot of coaches – myself included – will have leadoff hitters work to see a strike, and the reasoning here is to allow hitters to see as many pitches as possible, early in the game. This is not necessarily a guideline I coach by, but it's a strong consideration. Another example includes a pitcher fighting to find the strike zone, walking multiple hitters in a row. Conventional wisdom says to see a strike, however, that is also situational – score, who's hitting, who's coming up next, how many runners are on base, what inning is it? At more advanced levels, where scouting reports are necessary, coaches may have their hitters see more pitches the first time through an order.

If the first pitch is in a hitter's zone, tee off!

On-Deck Hitter – Purposeful, Not a Hang Out!

Conversation can be had within the dugout about pitching tendencies. The on-deck circle is not an area for a hitter to merely hang out. Before an at-bat, it is important for the batter to work on load and timing. The on-deck hitter is to use their time to prepare for their at-bat. Ideally, both the batter and on deck hitter are in sequence with their individual loads and timing to the ball. It's not necessary that a player swing while on deck.

PLATE COVERAGE

Hit it Where it's Pitched.

To the fault of nobody, growing up in 90s I had many coaches, from those I worked with at camps, to those that coached teams I was on, continue to force backside – opposite field. We've likely all been there. The coach begins a round of batting practice, and during one of those rounds you were "moving the runner," or, in other terms, hitting the ball to the opposite field. I had coaches adamantly tell us to hit backside on *any* pitch location. They taught us an "inside out" swing, and it forced players to drop their back shoulders and hands to force the ball to the right side, regardless of where the ball was actually pitched. The instruction here was to focus on staying inside of the ball. It is true that we should support hitters to attack the inside part of the ball; it keeps the bat head in the zone longer. But when forcing backside on inside pitches, you also lose extension, a major component in swing path. To hit opposite field on hard, inside pitches, you're forcing bat drag, and the front shoulder must open to push to the right side.

Players with great bat control let the ball get a little deeper, keep their hands inside the ball, and allow the bat head to stay in the zone long enough to get pitches on the middle part of the plate to go backside. But that forceful expectation of backside has gone away with the horse and buggy.

Hit it where it's pitched!

Forcing backside with hitters that do not have sufficient understanding of their swing can be highly counterproductive. To begin, hitters must be able to handle inside pitches, especially with increased velocity. We teach hitters to hit the inside pitch out in front, but also *used* to tell hitters to simultaneously go backside.

Having a backside approach is looking for a particular pitch location – middle/away. When you see teams at the college level hitting to the backside of second base, they're doing so based on pitch location in which they can handle the bat appropriately. In the drills' section of this book we'll focus on plate coverage repetitions to help promote a sound understanding. What we're looking for is a consistent swing that covers all parts of the plate. Take balls on the outer half to the opposite field, and pull hard inside pitches!

When teams hit behind runners, it's not because they're placing balls to right field regardless of where it's pitched. Instead, it has to do with *pitch selection*. This is an approach. The hitter's mindset is to now look to expand their zone to the outer half of the plate, hitting behind the runner. In situations where hitting behind the runner is necessary, the player's zone changes to pitches with which they can do so.

This has to be practiced! In the drills and team batting practice sections of this book, you will see drills and routines that promote pitch location and plate coverage. Coaches have to be mindful that our expectations are met through *practice*. If hitting routines do not include plate coverage, it's difficult to expect team members to do so with success. Drill work should include, in some capacity, hitting pitches inside and outside, with a lot of repetition designated to both. Then begins the progression of focusing on all pitches within hitting sessions – hard pull and backside approach, which leads to normal front toss with a combination of pitches. This can be achieved through tee work, side toss, and close front toss.

The above photos demonstrate the ball being hit on the inside part of the plate, as well as the outside part of the plate. Very little is different except where the ball is hit in association of depth traveled, and slight shoulder posture. As previously discussed, the contact point for an outside pitch is not beyond the hitter, as is often taught. This particular pitch was a well-hit line drive to left field.

COACHING HITTERS AND RUNNERS FROM THIRD BASE

Less is More.

We're coaches. It's what we do! We want to continually help our athletes be the best that they can. They need our guidance. We can see their swings. We can see their flaws. We want to help, to instruct, to run the game, and to impose runs and wins.

In regard to specific hitting mechanics, **in-game at-bats is absolutely not the time to explain to a hitter what they're doing wrong mechanically**. Kids have to compete and focus on approach, plate coverage, and pitch recognition. Hitting mechanics are adjusted – if necessary – during practice. It is discouraged during even pregame batting practice. Unless it's a very simple adjustment, I do not encourage the conversation to even be had in the dugout. Save it for practice.

Besides not wanting a player to overthink in the box, a coach must also understand an approach in helping through flaws. There have to be verbalizations, of course, but "fixing" a swing is done through an adequate progression of drills. We fix through purposeful reps more than we do our spoken words. With that consideration, now think of that player in the batters' box attempting to make three different mechanical adjustments during a live at-bat. Focusing on a particular body movement impedes a player's ability to focus on simply hitting the ball.

> *"At third base, I give signs, check the defense, and coach base runners that cannot see the ball. Few players ever hear hitting instruction from me during a game, and if they do it is very simple, such a reminder to be on time."*
>
> *Joe Abraham – Head Softball Coach,* University of Toledo

Keep It Simple:

Coaches must be themselves and use their strengths as a coach, and sometimes that means putting a little more pressure on players. That's perfectly acceptable, but I strongly recommend staying away from negative, condescending comments while a player is doing what is widely considered the most difficult thing in sports. Be uplifting, be positive, and allow them to have fun – even at advanced levels.

"Good BP swing here."

I use this vocal gesture a lot – almost every at-bat – in some form. It obviously depends on the situation, but before a player has two strikes, I want them to step into the box with the "BP" approach – attack their red zone. A BP swing does not indicate that the pitcher is throwing poorly. Instead, it reminds the player to focus on his or her zone.

"Make her come to you."

"Get your pitch."

"Has to be yours here."

All three of these verbal gestures, heard at basically every game in America all actually mean the same thing – approach. But these encouraging words lack value because they're said too often with so little meaning to the hitter. They're words that just roll off a coach's tongue, because it's simply expected that a coach is going to say something on every pitch, and that's just isn't necessary! Instead, consider, "BP swing only," for a more definitive, precise, better understood cue. If truly a batter "looks for their pitch" they are looking red zone – batting practice approach. Note: This is not to suggest only the given tips are to be used for your hitters. It's entirely up to the feel of the coach. The point, however, is to be clearer in communication with a hitter that is already under the pressure of hitting.

"Fastball and adjust. Keep competing!"

Chill Out!

As a young coach I was more animated at third base. My college coach taught us principles that carried over into our coaching careers, but I did have to make cognizant adjustments for hitters and base runners. Assertive, definitive vocalizations are encouraged. Yelling, shaking your head, throwing your hands up, and other dramatic hand gestures are all examples of poor body language, which negatively effects hitters. The same ideals can also be used on the bases. Limit body movements so that players have crystal clear guidance.

Above all, remain in control of your emotions. We expect our players to, and in high-intense moments of baseball and softball, the worst thing we can do for players is to allow ourselves to be overcome in the heat of the moment. The fans are going crazy. The ump made a bad call. Some fool in the stands is cursing. The opposing team's dugout is acting like caged animals. During these times it is critically important to remain composed for the hitter and base runners.

Base Runner Engagement:

While it's important to limit words with your hitter, the same can be said for base runners. Softball and baseball plays happen extremely fast, and once again, too many words and phrases can confuse the runner. There should be upmost importance put on proper base running. Losing runs because a player is not engaged or does not understand highly important base running situations results in lost games. This is part of a hitting book because they'll later be practiced during whole-team batting practice. Being a good base runner does not coincide with speed. Good base runners are engaged and fundamentally focused. Keep it simple:

- Have all base runners return the number of outs to the coach. The coach may flash that there are two outs, and the base runner should return the sign.
- The phrase, "Freeze on a line drive" is universal and *incorrect*. Its point is to teach young players not to take off on a line drive, but to actually freeze. In both baseball and softball, an *adequate* lead (and secondary) allows players throughout the field to back pick a runner. This should be completely unacceptable on your team! Instead, when a runner is on, the verbal cue is, "Check back on a line." On a line drive, the players' weight should shift to the return base while watching the ball through before advancing. As the ball appears to have a direct line to a defender, the player may take a step back toward the bag. It's all about good reads! When a player is halfway up the base path on a line drive, it shows lack of basic fundamental understanding, or worse, that they're checked out mentally.
- "At you or behind, you're here." This is the verbal cue given when a runner is at second base, with no runner on first. With good, quick reads – not delayed reads – runners in both baseball and softball should advance to third when the ball is hit on the ground directly at them, and obviously behind them (at second base, or on the left side of second base from runner's perspective).
- Players should also be taught to never round a bag if they're either not receiving an indicator by the coach to do so, or they do not know where the ball is. Especially on infield ground balls, good teams will have their players at first look back to the runner. For example, if a slow roller is hit with a runner on first, the defender may not be able to get the force out at second. They instead throw to first base. Rounding second base is dangerous as a base runner because a strong defense will be taught to throw behind the runner.
- As a third base coach, limit body movement if at all possible. As runners advance, a team should have very set routines. If the third base coach is down the line, the runner is thinking of only one thing – scoring. Because a coach is going to be down the line, reading the ball, it is possible that they will have the runner return at the last moment. As the runner is closely watching their

coach, it can cause confusion if there are too many movements. When I coach third base, I am pointing home with my right hand, while motioning with my left. If I am going to stop them, both hands go up. This seems simple enough, but as the coach is watching the ball, I have witnessed the coach's hands beginning to slow down because they begin to doubt themselves. As a result, the runner slows down. Reprimand ensues and I have empathy for the base runners that stop or slow down at third. Reduce movements, and **define them at practice**!

- If possible, take a knee at third base when you want an on-coming runner to slide. Kneel to the left or right side of the base, and coach players to slide at you – an inside or outside slide.
- Reading the ball up or down at third base is more important than any other bag. The first move on a ball hit upward is always back! This is not a check back; your body is moving back to the bag. Once the ball is through the infield, the runner is scoring easily even if they're standing on third base. There should be no risk in being back picked, or being too far off that you cannot score. The same goes for deep fly balls. The runner must see it either caught or down before advancing because if the ball is hit deep into the outfield, the runner can jog in for the score. But if a great play is made and the runner "thought" the ball was down, they are risking an unnecessary return, and therefore a lost run. Even on "no doubt" homeruns, return! See it over the fence, jog home, and meet your teammate. **A great catch should never ruin a scoring opportunity in the outfield. Guarantee it!**
- Runners read the *defender and the ball* in fly ball situations. Their body language tells more than the flight of the ball alone.
- The on-deck hitter is the third coach. If there is a play at home, the on deck-hitter should position themselves behind the plate to communicate sliding inside or outside, or to remain up.

Condition players to be self-aware on the bases. The reality is that once the ball is in play, a verbal command from a coach is likely too late. Obviously there are times when a player must be dependent upon the coach because they're not able to see the ball, but base running is much more self-reliant than some think. One example is a passed ball. This is a yes or no decision – nothing in between. If the coach has to tell the runner at third to advance, they are significantly later than if they reacted immediately.

<u>Coaching from Third Base Review:</u>

- **Don't teach hitting mechanics**
- **Limit verbal cues for hitters and runners**
- **You don't have to talk every pitch**
- **Define your routines with clarity and practice them**

DRILLS WITH PURPOSE

The following drills are to serve as a guideline. These are drills I have used with great effectiveness, and with the feedback from other trusted coaches at a high level. As with any position and any sport, drills must have a purpose. Implementing drills as time fillers and without fundamental understanding will not only lack in purpose, but it will also hinder the development of hitters. The rationale and intricacies of each drill are to be taken seriously.

There are dozens upon dozens of quality drills. The following drills hardly scratch the surface but should help build as a solid foundation to use as part of batting practice and individualized work. *All drills can be altered or made individual depending on a player's strengths, weaknesses, and overall ability.* There are times when a player should just hit – smash the ball. But we cannot neglect what they'll see in games, too. Make adjustments so players must cover the strike zone and work various approaches. **Making adjustments** could be quite simple – adjustment in tee or pitch location.

Sexy Drills – Buyer Beware:

You can find drills with a simple internet search. If you have social media and follow various softball or baseball groups, you've likely seen drills plastered all over your feed. Some are great, and some simply look "sexy." Those types of drills are the ones that *appear* cool. They may appease parents sitting in the stands, look cool to the players, and falsely show this deep understanding of efficient hitting practice. Be careful. Hitting is fun! Most kids enjoy solid contact. Sometimes, that's all we need. Simply put, don't over-think hitting drills and fall for ones that look really neat but lack purpose and value.

While I was watching an MLB game, I heard broadcasters outline a particular player's pregame routine. For the first few cuts, the player was swinging in more of a golf style – feet were planted and there was no weight shift. The purpose was to utilize hands within parts of the zone, remaining inside of the ball, as well as core use. The point is, we must have rationale behind all drills. That particular drill was *for that particular player*, not implemented for the whole team without purpose.

Always ask yourself the intent of your drill and be specific in your response.

- What is this drill helping?
- What is its goal?
- What happens after this drill?
- Is it a realistic swing or does it alter mechanics?

We also have responsibility, as coaches, to put accountability on the player to do the drill right. Effective drills are only effective when executed correctly. For example, if a player is hitting off the tee and working on a particular plate location, *every* swing must be with intent and purpose. Haphazardly swinging or otherwise goofing around is worse than not taking any reps at all. Hitting is hard. Drills must be done correctly. It's ok to take breaks, too: if a player is tired, rest!

> *"Drills are a process of feel, to a real swing."*
> *Keith Werman - Development Coordinator,* San Diego Padres

Mechanics – Keep Them Consistent:

Regardless of the drill presented, mechanics should not change! Some of the more difficult drills – top/bottom hand swing – can pose problems, especially with young players that are not strong enough to handle the bat with one hand. In such cases, you must ask yourself if the drill is of benefit or simply being conducted without purpose. Always evaluate both hitter and yourself.

Tee Work is Not Tee Ball:

Tee work is one of the most common drills, for youth through elite Major League hitters. That, too, must be purposeful. Visualize a pitcher, move to the load/launch position, and swing through the ball as if it were pitched. Remaining focused on only the ball throughout all tee work is not as effective as also including visualization, which is simulation of a pitched ball.

1. Tee Drill

1. The batter begins in their normal hitting stance, with their eyes focused on a visualized pitcher.
2. Load as normal, and hit the ball with intent and reasonable aggression.
3. Repeat, but be purposeful and slow. Do not rush repetitions.

Goal: The goal of this drill is quite simple. The player should be aware of their basic body mechanics through feel. Hitting the ball with a slight upward launch is the desired path; get even to the ball on the swing path. A basic tee drill can be used for a variety of reasons, and if there is an empty field or batting tunnel, its effectiveness can be stretched to achieve various flights of the ball. For example, repeating tee work with the purpose of hitting the top back of the cage is repeating bat path and launch angle. Be sure to hit high and low pitches, as well. Adjust the tee to cover all parts of the strike zone, not just one, middle location.

An emphasis on high pitches can teach the hitter to get on plane and also prevent heavy back shoulder dipping. Another variation that can be fun for players is to put another tee 20-40 feet in front of the hitter, with a ball. The hitter's job is to hit their ball off of the tee in order to knock the ball off the tee placed in front. Elevate the tee to promote line drives/launch angles. This takes a great deal of concentration.

2. Three-Position Tee Drill

1. Similar to regular tee work, the player will simulate and visualize.
2. Depending upon the location of the tee, the player makes contact at the appropriate location:
   - Away – deep in the zone, at roughly the same depth as the front leg
   - Middle – middle of the plate
   - Inside – in front of the plate, with extension
3. Remember that mechanics do not change. Be aware of players dipping to hit the outside pitch. The bat path does not change for inside/outside pitches, and *contact points are dependent upon the player's swing.*

Goal: The goal of a three-position tee is to repeat various pitch locations at a relatively high rate. For players demonstrating weakness in plate coverage, the three-position tee drill may be the first step in the progression.

3. Three Step Tee Drill

1. Assuming a right-handed hitter, the player is three steps back from the plate.
2. The player steps once with their right foot, then with their left, and finally with their right foot.
3. At the point in which the right foot steps forward a second time, they are now in a balanced, launch position.
4. From this position there is a slight weight distribution to the back side along with hand separation. With a light front foot step, swing normally, from the load position. **Avoid an exaggerated backside lean, but there should be a weight transfer to the front side.**

Goal: The goal of this drill is also for feel – slight negative movement (load and weight distribution to the backside). It is also a good drill for hitters that are "loud" in the box. Players that have excessive movements such as happy feet or a definitive hitch will benefit from this drill. We want hitters to be quiet at especially the backside of the load. Looseness, balance, and steadiness in the swing allows for quick hands and a smooth path to the ball.

4. Top Hand/Bottom Hand Tee Drill

1. As with normal tee work, the player is visualizing and focused on a simulated pitch.
2. With one hand, go through normal swing mechanics, including the load.
3. Swing the bat with high-intent contact, focusing on a consistent bat path – same as a normal swing.

Goal: The goal of focusing on top and bottom hand only is to isolate the swing mechanics to a more singular look – one arm at a time. It is absolutely top priority that the bat path and other body mechanics do not change. Choking up on the bat will be required. Coaches should not force players to swing with more weight than they can handle to adequately swing through the zone. The progression of this drill is likely to begin tee work, then move into normal swinging. Most players swing with their bottom hand without problems. When they swing with their top hand it must be observed if it's being done correctly. Players have a tendency to swing with all arm, ignoring their core. The swing does not change! For young athletes, the coach must keep a watchful eye on this drill. Top hand/bottom hand drills can also be used for side toss and front toss.

5. Side Toss Drill

1. As with tee drills, the hitter is in a balance, pre-pitch stance with their eyes forward, visualizing a pitcher.
2. The partner is on one knee, feeding the ball to the hitter's desired zone.
3. To begin the process, the partner begins with his or her hand elevated. They then drop their hand before bringing it back up to its release point.
    o Instead of simply tossing it, it's important to drop the hand from a higher starting point to allow for a load. This is important for side toss!
4. The player will hit the ball with intent, depending on the desired plate location of the pitch.
5. The feeder can work an inside, middle, or outside focus.

Goal: This drill is pretty self-explanatory and nearly every team at every level understands side toss. The coaching point here is intent. Tell your players to not take weak, lazy swings. As with tee work, we are looking to hit the ball with authority. Do not rush pitches for "speed reaction." There is little value in that and it often creates bad habits. Some refer to this as rapid fire. That does not increase bat speed.

6. Sitting Front Toss Drill – Plate Coverage

1. The feeder is on a bucket or chair, seated within close proximity to the hitter, behind adequate protection.
2. The feeder brings their hand back to allow for a hitting load.
3. The feeder throws the ball repeatedly to a designated location – inside/outside focus.
4. The hitter repeats middle/back approach, or a hard pull.

Goal: This drill is part of a progression, not an isolated drill in itself. We want hitters to feel comfortable letting balls get deeper, in a middle/away approach, while also handling the bat with quickness and aggression on the inner half of the plate. When I do this drill, I do not mix them; that will come later in the workout. Instead, I focus on hit balls only as hard pull, then only as middle/away. Focus on bat path and plate coverage.

7. 0-2 Approach, Sitting Front Toss

1. Similar to sitting front toss, the thrower is in close proximity to the hitter.
2. Upon the thrower bringing their arm back, the hitter begins their load.
3. The thrower throws the ball with relatively high velocity, or they lob the ball.
4. The hitter looks fastball, and adjusts to off speed.

Goal: Initially, this drill is difficult. You should be able to see an increase in concentration and bat speed throughout the process of this drill, but do not expect players to master it immediately. The player is to look fastball and adjust to off-speed. Balance is a focus area here; they should not be lunging in anticipation of a fastball. The thrower may have to reduce speed or adjust their distance. It is expected to be challenging, but not impossible. This, too, is part of a progression. When throwing live BP rounds, one of the rounds can focus on a high-velocity, 0-2 approach. Bat speed is not only a physical ability; it is also a mental approach.

8. Walk Up Drill:

1. The batter begins at the first plate and takes a determined amount of swings, as few as one.
2. After a swing attempt – or a predetermined successful rep – the batter moves to the next plate.
3. Repeat through all three plates, progressing toward the thrower, or the desired, set routine.
   - The player can begin anywhere. They could start close and move back, or begin in the middle and move back before moving forward – anything.

Goal: The purpose of this drill is pitch recognition and timing. As you move closer, the reaction time obviously decreases. Pitches can also be thrown off-speed. This drill is a good hitters' count drill – sit red zone – or a good 2 strike drill – fastball and adjust.

9. Batting Practice, Front Toss:

I believe that the majority of practice swings should come by way of normal front toss. The options here are quite unlimited, but the focus must include *purpose* and *intent*. Within normal BP, here are example focus areas:

- **Hitter's count** – hit the ball hard in your red zone. *Every* swing should result in solid contact.
- **Hit it where it's pitched** – Focus on inside pull and middle/away dependent upon where the ball is thrown. Hitters can look dead pull and/or middle away for every pitch, or mix it up to cover the plate at random.

- **0-2 approach with high velocity** – throw a bit harder and include off speed pitches. The hitter is looking fastballs and adjusting to off speed, keeping in mind good mechanics and avoiding lunging.
- **Kill round** – YES! Without changing mechanics, it's ok to think aggressively. It is ok to have players think homerun and "smoked" gap shots. The "kill round" should be low repetitions due to its physical demand. The round is a mentality; sit on your red zone pitch and hit it out. I use phrases such as, "Hit the ball through the screen," or "Ruin this ball." I like this approach because it precludes thinking: **the only objective is to hit the ball hard.**
- **Cover K zone** – with this focus the player is swinging at almost every pitch. This may work well for hitters who lack aggressiveness and/or do not understand their attack zone. The focus here is to hit every single ball in the strike zone, so the thrower must locate well. Coaches develop more through doing, and this drill can be a good confidence boost for those with plate apprehension.

A Note on Pitching Machine Use:

With technology advances, some types of pitching machines can throw a particular pitch with a push of a button. Pitching machines have their use – particular pitch location, high velocity, bunting, and defensive focuses, such as catcher receiving. In general, however, pitching machines should be used at minimum. Poor-quality machines are not realistic enough to allow for hitters to load properly, oftentimes leading to lunging and poor timing. This serves no benefit, and it can, in fact, have adverse results. Machine use must allow for purpose.

Weighted Bat Use:

Stay with the theme – purpose. The use of a weighted bat can be beneficial for more advanced players that can develop self-feel. As a catching instructor, I often use weighted balls for receiving/framing work. If you do not receive the ball appropriately, you have instant feedback. Catchers that are taught proper technique, including meeting the ball and not dropping the fingers downward for throwing-side pitches, can self-evaluate with drills that use weighted balls. With a weighted ball, it must be caught correctly or the glove will be manipulated out of the strike zone. Using a weighted bat for drill work serves the same purpose.

> *"Using a heavy bat allows players to feel mechanics and figure it out on their own. Use of high velocity in combination of a weighted bat offers that feedback."*
> *Keith Werman – Development Coordinator,* San Diego Padres

"I think one of the greatest challenges coaches today face is individualizing hitting instruction in a team setting. Most coaches use a series of drills for the entire unit. Oftentimes, it really benefits about a third of the team and sets back about a third. The best coaches in the system can bring the middle third up to the top, but in the best case it only benefits about two thirds. I challenge all coaches to learn the individual player and come up with a developmental plan for each individual. That's when everyone can improve. That's what I feel the best coaches can do – help the individual maximize his or her swing while also helping to prepare them to win in the batter's box mentally. There are two components and every player is different."

Bill Cilento – Associate Head Coach, Wake Forest University

In the coming pages you will read a framework to help with both individual and team hitting. The most critical aspect is to understand team and individual needs. To Coach Cilento's point, it does not necessarily mean that you have 15-25 players doing completely different drills. What it does mean, however, is that each player may have a slightly different focus or approach within a drill and/or batting practice focus. For example, two players working in one station on a tee may have different work to do. One player may be working to keep his or her hands above the ball, utilizing high tee work, while the other is using the three-step tee drill to help with balance and quietness of the load. The options are there, but differences in hitting work does not have to be drastic.

Drills at a Glance:

- **What is the drill's purpose?**
- **What part of a progression is the drill?**
- **Does the swing focus on mechanics and approach that is consistent with in-game swings?**

INDIVIDUAL WORK

Do More, Talk Less. No Gimmicks and Quick Fixes.

Please don't tell someone they have a "simple fix." That is gimmicky and in athletics, there are no successful gimmicks. Even the simplest mechanical flaws must be accompanied by purposeful drill work and progression. Is their timing off? Is there a hitch that makes them late? Are they off balance? Verbalizing a mechanical flaw to a player and expecting it to be "fixed" is faulty coaching. Even at the collegiate level, where players should be accountable for self-improvement, you cannot expect them to hear a verbalized "fix" and adjust immediately. When we're talking *approach*, that's something that can serve as a simple reminder, therefore a "fix." Hold players accountable to continue individual work on their own, but don't leave them hanging with a few confusing verbalized (and oftentimes jargon-filled) phrases.

Oftentimes mechanical flaws first begin with the stance, so if a coach rambles on about three different imperfections it demonstrates a lack of knowledge in where hitting starts – the stance. Remember that from a balanced stance we must have a swing path that is on an even plane to the pitched ball, keep the bat in the zone, and cover all parts of the plate. As we work from the ground up, many flaws are as a result of this domino effect.

There are no simple fixes. If it were that easy, we would all be making a lot of money teaching professional hitters.

Simplify. Don't Confuse.

Hitting is one of the easiest concepts in sports. Hit the ball with the bat. It's also simultaneously the most difficult thing to do in sports. Complicating a swing, especially for a hitter with flaws, is worse than not making corrections. Fewer words. Fewer adjustments. Positive reps. And remember that all swings are different, so an adjustment made for one player may not necessarily work for another. There are absolutes in hitting and swing mechanics, but getting there looks different for many.

The majority of individual hitting workouts I do have limited mechanical adjustments. There must be an obvious flaw that prohibits the ability to hit with purpose before I start changing too much. Subtle adjustments, usually through drill work, happen much more frequently than major changes. Every hitter, regardless of the level, has periodic flaws in their swing. That could literally change from pitch to pitch. If we focus too much on perfecting a swing after every pitch we lose focus on what's really important.

See the big picture before determining a direction, and that direction will not always be the same for every player.

Just as there are some absolutes in hitting mechanics, there are also absolutes in the *why* of hitting flaws. From dipping to lunging, to casting the hands to having a stiff load, many mechanical issues can be solved through a progression of specific drills, with adjustments. However, I do not believe in a particular blue print to fix mechanical issues for players I *do not see*. It isn't always that simple. Suzy's lunge could be very different than Timmy's, and the approach to adjust could vary. Therefore, putting together a list of adjustments is not something I feel to be beneficial, especially without actually seeing the player hit. It would be like a doctor making a diagnosis based on what is most likely seen, versus an actual exam of that patient to actually verify.

Significant Changes – One Example:

Years ago I coached a travel team and within that team each player had four individual workouts. Some of the players' hitting mechanics were adjusted slightly, but few were drastic, and adjustments were made through drills more so than verbalizations. One such player was having difficulty hitting during normal BP due to seriously flawed mechanics. He faced the following issues:

- His weight started on the backside, with heavy lean.
- With the exception of the backside weight, there was no flex in his stance – no athleticism.
- His hands were above the shoulders, already in a stiff, poor load position – no negative movement to promote looseness of hands and proper swing path. His swing path started directly from the stance, causing an initial hand drop that began forward movement.
- Upon swinging, his feet had an exaggerated lunge, dropping his eyes significantly, and his hands dropped below his shoulders, from the hard bottom hand pull of the bat.

Suffice it to say that this swing was completely prohibitive. The flaws were far too much to work through by way of simple drills, and certainly through verbalizations. **So, we made adjustments to his stance to *simplify* his swing**:

- We widened his base and put flex into his knees to be more athletic, and balanced. Widening the base, for this particular player *(Not for everyone!)* was implemented to reduce movement. His feet were similar to Jeff Bagwell's, although not quite as widened.
- Before the pitcher came set, the player rested the bat on their shoulder – preload approach.

- When the pitcher came set, the hitter lifted the bat off of his shoulder. This intent was to keep the bat quiet with less movement in the load – lift, then load.
- Upon the pitch, the load was simplified. Also similar to Jeff Bagwell, for weight transfer he had a subtle left foot (front side) lift. Because the bat was positioned on the shoulder, after lifting the bat head, the load only required a slight bottom hand push to accomplish the 45 degree angle.
- These adjustments served several purposes – limiting movement, developing a compact swing, and minimizing the strike zone, while also targeting their red zone.

The results ended up working well for this young man, and shortly thereafter he enjoyed a significantly improved success rate in hitting. But that was NOT an "easy fix." In fact, we had to revisit its purpose multiple times throughout the rest of the season. Oftentimes, that review was to slow down, revisit the tee and continue a progression of drills – high purpose repetitions.

There are no easy fixes.
Everyone's swing is different.

The following workouts are not intended for easy fixes, and they should be *adjusted for the individual*, if necessary. My goal in describing these workouts is to help develop individual coach's ideas. Coaches must adjust as necessary and understand their players in order to implement proper drill routines. The following drill work is a guide. Use it, but make adjustments to the benefit of the individual. Throughout these types of workouts, there are various talking points; it's not just pedal to the metal.

Focus = habits. In my career, one of major emphasis I have found critical is that of focus. It seems simple: focus and you'll do well. Sometimes instead of a swing flaw there needs to be a mental concentration and accountability.

Limit swings during sessions! The workouts can be in excess of 100 swings, but there must be breaks and change in pace. Absolutely do not allow for a hitter to take dozens of swings without breaks and intent. For one live drill or batting practice session, I do not go beyond 15 – and that's on the high end – in any round.

Hitting Lessons and Workouts – Basic Format:

Objective: To increase player hitting potential through a progression, with focus on:

- Plate coverage
- Pitch recognition
- Hitter's count approach
- Competitive 0-2 approach w/ fastball look

- Developing a bat path to the same plane as the ball
- Competitive nature – barrel it up!

BREAKS! Hitters should not be hitting excessive amounts of pitches without breaks. Repetition amounts vary depending on the player.

*BP toss – Standing at what would be considered normal batting practice distance.

*Bucket/chair – These drills are up close to focus very specifically, with a high number of reps, with controlled location.

Workout #1

- Bunting – full bucket, left/right
- Warm up round – normal BP
- Plate coverage, close up (toss from chair/bucket)
  - Hard inside pull
  - Outside coverage, backside and middle
- 0-2 approach, (toss from chair bucket)
- 0-2 high velo with off speed (BP tosses)
- Backside/middle approach (pitch recognition – normal BP tosses)
- BP approach – concentration round. All balls barreled up well.
- Kill round

Workout #2

- Bunting – full bucket
- Warm up round
- Inside, hard pull, BP toss
- Backside/middle approach, BP toss
- High velo, all fastball. Bat speed focus, BP toss
- 0-2 approach, high velo with off speed, BP toss
- Kill round
- Competitive hitting round
  - Bunting, x10
  - Hitters count, x5
  - Backside/middle, x5

- o   Plate coverage, x5
- o   0-2 with off speed, x5
  - ▪   30 total points

Workout #3

- •   Bunt bucket
- •   12-rep focus with breaks, BP toss
  - o   BP
  - o   Backside
  - o   High velo
  - o   0-2 high velo with off speed
  - o   Kill round
- •   Repeat one time
- •   Competitive hitting
  - o   Bunting, x10
  - o   Hitters count, x5
  - o   Backside/middle, x5
  - o   Plate coverage, x5
  - o   0-2 with off speed, x5
    - ▪   30 total points

Workout #4

- •   Between the cones – bunting successfully
- •   8-rep focus, BP toss
  - o   BP
  - o   Backside
  - o   High velo
  - o   0-2 high velo with off speed
  - o   Kill round
- •   Repeat two times
- •   Competitive Hitting
  - o   Bunting, x10
  - o   Hitters count

- o Backside/middle
- o Plate coverage
- o 0-2 with off speed
    - 30 total points

"Coaches and hitters need to build a routine for the process of improvement."
Derrick May – Former Major League Baseball player and coach

"We are in the era of a swing coach, not a hitting coach. We need more hitting coaches. A coach that can do both – biomechanics and teach how to hit – are elite."
Bill Cilento – Associate Head Baseball Coach, Wake Forest University

BATTING PRACTICE WITH A PURPOSE

Movement and Pace, with Defense and Base Running

Coaches should always try to limit how much players are stationary during practice. Batting practice can be *extremely* boring, slowing down the pace of the practice significantly, and generally putting everyone to sleep. Baseball and softball are games of habit. It's about positive, productive repetitions, and a batting practice routine should include multiple aspects of the game, including hitting, defense, and base running. The following can be used as a practice routine as well as a pre-game hitting routine.

This again is to serve as a guide, not a blue print. For younger kids, it has to be dialed down significantly from this plan. But have a plan. Have purpose. Limit standing around.

During Whole-team Batting Practice, be Mindful of:

- Short purposeful hitting rounds, limiting laborious periods of time and long at-bats.
- Keeping groups small. There should not be a line of hitters merely standing around awaiting their turn.
- Defensive purpose.
- A base running component within batting practice.
- Assume a group of five hitters. Two begin hitting while three practice base running. When the first two hitters complete their first round, they go through their base running responsibilities.

Whole Team Batting Practice Plan

Defensive Focus:

The defense should not be used to simply get the balls back to the pitcher! There are various set-ups that can be used successfully, depending on team needs and the availability of proper equipment. Follow the defensive responsibilities and formats:

- A bucket should be placed as an easy collection point, oftentimes directly behind or in front of second base. Again, this depends on the focus. If all ground balls are to be thrown to second base to simulate a double play, protective fencing should be in front of second base, with the bucket.

- If a position has multiple players, they should take turns fielding off of the batted ball.
- If numbers allow, defensive players should only field *from their position*. For example, if the shortstop reacts to a ball hit deep to their right, every effort should be made to successfully field the ball. If the next batted ball is then hit to their left, *before they were able to return to position,* the fielder should ignore it.
- Balls should not be thrown across the diamond unless first base has a protective screen in front of them. Players can instead field, set their feet, and then return the balls to bucket location. Allowing infield throws slows down the routine significantly.
- If available, another coach should hit groundballs and/or fly balls between hitting reps. This keeps the defense moving and increases the amount of repetitions.

Base Running Reads:

Base running is an area of the sport that is often neglected, especially given that it has many intricacies so crucial to a successful offense. Fundamental base running is so often the difference in wins and losses! What better time to get purposeful reps than during whole-team batting practice? During batting practice, base runners are working on their reads. Consider this "station to station". The base runners only advance to the next base. The same base running principles previously discussed should be applied with very specific concentration. Since runners are going from base-to-base, a coach is not necessary at third base.

- Each hitter within the hitting group will begin on first base before taking their cuts, except the player (or first two) that bats first; they'll go through the bases once their first round is complete.
- Players are focusing on reads, and the coach can have players simulate differently – nobody else is on (even if there is a runner in front or behind), or play it as the runners get on base, simulating normal play.
- Assume less than two outs.
- If the ball is hit deep into the outfield, the runner should either consider a tag, or get off the bag as far as they can to safely return to the bag. This is NOT a "ho hum" procedure! Players should be moving full speed.
- On line drives, players "check back". As discussed previously, and often said at especially Little League levels as the "rule," to freeze on a line drive is poor base running.
- When advancing home during batting practice, runners simulate advancing before veering into foul territory.
- Once they have completed all bases, they are to begin preparing for their hitting rounds. Hitters only run the bases once.

- This focus is all about **base runner reads and focus**. Runners are reading ball up, ball down, and location.

I do not believe proper base running is emphasized or practiced enough with purpose and efficiency. Simply running the bases because it happens to be a player's or group's turn is not enough. Base running should be a highly focused part of practice, integrated with other skill areas simultaneously.

Hitting Routine:

The intent, amount of swings, and pace is totally dependent upon the level and needs of the team. There should be focus within each round, but that could be as simple as attacking pitches in the strike zone to develop plate discipline with younger hitters. Each round is suggested to be 8-10 swings, and it should not exceed 12.

Round One:
- Three bunts third base, three bunts first base.
  - Coaches can also consider having a bunting station behind the hitter, if proper protective screening is available. Base runners should simulate their read, but not carry out to the advancing base.
- Normal BP round – swing away within the red zone attack.

Round Two:
- Middle/away. Hitters are hitting pitches they can handle to the middle of the field and backside. Hitters should not swing at any pitches tight and inside. Remember that a backside approach is about *pitch selection*, not forcing inside pitches to the opposite field.

Round Three:
- Hit it where it's pitched. Hitters hard pull inside pitches and use the middle/backside of the field for pitches on the middle and outer-half of the plate. This is for *pitch recognition.*

Round Four:
- Attack red zone. Hitters should be aggressive on pitches within their individual red zone. Balls should be hit with authority into the gaps, and at advanced levels, this is often the round when balls are hit out. This is not an over-swing; it is a hitter's count round in which the hitter is prepared to attack pitches in their zone.

Other focuses can include an 0-2 count. Here, the coach throwing batting practice can change speeds, or keep the velocity consistent. The hitter still does not swing at pitches out of the zone but should work to cover all parts of the plate. This is similar to round three – cover the K zone.

Sample Team Practice Plans

Coaches have to be organized with their practice plans. While coaches may find it necessary to deviate from a plan – we always do – not having a plan in itself is bad. It does not matter how young players are; organization is imperative in practice planning. I encourage coaches to put a posted plan outside of the dugout for players to see as they enter. Some coaches even post it outside of the complex so parents that may be in attendance can see the day's plan.

This should not be limited due to age. Players appreciate the organizational aspect, as well as seeing the "work" that is necessary. Some may argue that the players should just adjust accordingly and be ready for anything. That's ridiculous. *Coaches* adjust based on the feedback players are providing by their execution, but there is no reason for a player not to prepare via a practice plan. It also helps to keep practice moving efficiently. The following are three different practice plans, to be seen *as examples* of effective practice plans.

Practice Plan Sample 1

Game talking points and highlights: 4:00 – 4:10
Warm Up Routine: 4:10 – 4:25
Hitting focus day – Rotations: 4:25 – 5:10

- Outside of cage, station 1: Tee work (coach determines type)
- Outside of cage, station 2: Bunting
- Cage 1, station 3: Focus rotation (0-2, inside/outside pitch selection, or coach's choice)
- Cage 2, station 4: BP toss

BP routine, groups of five w/ runners: 5:15 – 5:50

- Middle/away pitch selection, x8
- Plate coverage, hit it where it's pitched, x8
- Red zone, x8

Pressure situation – Nobody on, nobody out, tie game. 5:55-6:05pm (Team competitions' chapter)

Clean up responsibilities: 6:05 – 6:15

Coach's Note: It is natural for coaches to discuss a game directly following a game, but stay brief. It is best to address areas the next day in practice to help set the tone, and allows for a period of deeper reflection rather than knee-jerk reactions.

Sample Practice Plan 2

Warm Up Routine: 4:00 – 4:15
Base running. Discuss "check back", most important at 3B: 4:15 – 4:45

- Home to first, break down
- First to third, picking up 3B coach
- Leads, secondary—aggressive, smart, purposeful
- Pitcher reads/steals (baseball only)
    - Front shoulder read, RHP   (Live pitcher simulation)
    - Left shoulder read, LHP   (Live pitcher simulation)

PFP (Pitcher Fielder Practice): 4:45 – 5:00

- Come backers (Step and throw/run it over, under hand)
- 4/3-1's (Pitchers move to their left on all balls on the ground to their left. 2B, 1B, and pitcher communication and cover practice.)

*Break
Defensive/Hitting focus, teams of two—primary OF/IF: 5:05 – 6:00

Hitting: Coach A
- BP Approach
- Side toss
- Bunting
- 0-2 approach (Nothing changes except plate coverage)

Infield: Coach B and Coach C
- Double plays
  - 543, 643, 463
  - Correct footwork, transfer, quickness opposed to arm strength
- Slow rollers
- 1B balls in dirt—scoop or body
- Infield pop-up priority and communication

Outfield: Coach B and Coach C
- OF angles
  - Charge and react
  - Stationary and react
- Anti-drift
  - Tennis ball drill
- Wide receiver drill—set feet!
- Priority drill (players are grouped short and deep for communication)

Infield/Outfield (Catchers will gear up): 6:00 – 6:10
Clean up responsibilities: 6:10-6:20

Coach's Note: This practice is based on rotations, starting with hitting. Coach A is in the batting cage with the outfielders, while coaches B and C work with the infield. Going off the completion of hitting practice, the team rotates infield to the cage and outfield back on the field. In this case, coaches B and C remain on the field. 55 minutes is used to complete two rotations.

Sample Practice Plan 3

Warm Up Routine, with diamond drill: 4:00 – 4:15
Defensive Focus: 4:15 – 5:00

Infield
- Angles – get deep!
- Slow rollers
- Infield Circus

Outfield
- Shallow fly focus – break and collect, slide forward, catch normal
- Breaking the perimeter – no steps. Collect and throw
- Communication drill

Catchers and pitchers
- Pregame routine, 15 minutes
- Pitchers throw to catchers

Extended I/O with pop-up priority: 5:05 – 5:30
Team BP w/ hitting groups: 5:35 – 6:10

- BP approach – attack red zone. Rounds of 8, 5, 3

Clean up responsibilities: 6:10 – 6:20

The Diamond Drill:

The diamond is one of my personal favorites. Position the team on a diamond. If you're inside, especially in a gym, use the area under both baskets and on both half-court lines, out of bounds for four equal groups. Begin with the ball at home, or if in a gym, under one hoop. The player throws across the diamond/gym, and runs to his or her right. The player receiving then throws that player out, and runs to his or her right. The game resumes at coach's discretion. Players will initially have difficulty with this drill until they begin to pick up the patterns. They will always throw either in front, or to their left. Keep it simple – catch the ball, throw the runner out, and run to your right. For younger ages, I suggest using a safety ball, or even a tennis ball to begin the game. All players' heads should be up at all times! Make your players sprint; this is a high-intense drill. No matter the age, it is best to begin with a walk through – several throws' worth at very slow speed. Players should be instructed that transfer and quickness matter most, not throwing velocity.

Infield Circus:

Infield circus is mentioned in Sample Practice Plan 3. There are variations of the structured routine, but its primary intent is to practice a high number of groundballs in a short amount of time. The following explains one variation of the routine, and coaches must keep in mind that this is a relatively high-intense, taxing drill. Breaks will be required. In this structure, three coaches are needed. Ideally, three people

receiving balls for the coaches is necessary. I do not encourage using players – oftentimes catchers – to stand around and catch for a coach, but sometimes it's necessary. If a coach can utilize more hands, it does allow for more purpose. This could include parent volunteers, student assistants, or maybe PO's (pitcher only).

Three coaches are stationed around home plate. One coach is to the left of home plate (left side of right-handed batters' box), one on or near home plate, and the other to the right of home plate (right side of the left-handed batters' box). Consider these coaches A, B, and C, from left to right. In this sample, assume one person to catch for the coach, as well. If resources are not available to have one receiver for each coach, players can simply toss the ball back to the hitting coach.

The infielders are positioned as normal and three coaches/hitters are to hit simultaneously so that each position is fielding. Each _set_ should be between two to five minutes, depending on the number of players and level of play. Five minutes for an infield with only one player at each position is quite a lot. For each groundball without a throw, be sure players are still setting their feet toward first/second base. _Each set is repeated until the determined time is **completed**._ For example, each set listed is three minutes. Coaches A, B, and C simply keep hitting groundballs until three minutes is complete.

Round One: (Three minutes per set)

Set One
1. Coach A hits to 3B. 3B throws to 1B. 1B returns the ball to Coach A.
2. Coach B hits to shortstop. Shortstop returns the ball to Coach B.
3. Coach C hits to 2B and 2B returns the ball to Coach C.

Set Two
1. Coach A hits to 3B. 3B returns the ball to Coach A.
2. Coach B hits to shortstop. Shortstop throws to 1B. 1B returns the ball to Coach B.
3. Coach C hits to 2B. 2B returns the ball to Coach C.

Set Three
1. Coach A hits to 3B. 3B returns the ball to Coach A.
2. Coach B hits the ball to shortstop. Shortstop returns the ball to Coach B.
3. Coach C hits the ball to 2B. 2B throws to 1B. 1B returns the ball to Coach C.

Break

Round Two:

Set One
1. Coach A hits to 3B. 3B throws to 2B, covering the bag. 2B returns the ball to Coach A.
2. Coach B hits to shortstop. Shortstop returns the ball to Coach B.
3. Coach C hits the ball to 1B. 1B returns the ball to Coach C.

Set Two
1. Coach A hits to 3B. 3B returns the ball to Coach A.
2. Coach B hits to shortstop. Shortstops feeds 2B at the bag. 2B returns the ball to Coach B.
3. Coach C hits to 1B. 1B returns the ball to Coach C.

Set Three
1. Coach A hits to 3B. 3B returns the ball to Coach A.
2. Coach B hits to 2B. 2B feeds shortstop, who is covering the bag. Shortstop returns the ball to Coach B.
3. Coach C hits to 1B. 1B returns the ball to Coach C.

Set Four
1. Coach A hits to 3B. 3B returns the ball to Coach A.
2. Coach B hits to 2B. 2B returns the ball to Coach B.
3. Coach C hits to 1B. 1B throws to shortstop, covering the bag. Shortstop returns the ball to Coach C.

Coaches are always seeking drills to help develop players. But we, as leaders of youth, have to understand that drills in isolation is not enough. I feel that far too often, drills that have "the look" are implemented without purpose. What structures and routines follow the drill? In the sample practice plans, each of them has a progression, from cage to on-field hitting, and infield/outfield drills to full-team IO. This brings everything together, and the focus of the previous drills should be carried over.

The more movement, the better. Some standing around is almost unavoidable. If players are consistently not moving for over one minute at a time, make strong considerations on how to keep them involved.

What about the outfield, a position that seems to get the least amount of purposeful repetitions that are not so redundant? A variation of infield circus could also work with the outfielders throwing to various bases. Here, the infield would also have responsibility to body up the ball and make an appropriate tag.

Because there are three hitters around home plate, plays at the plate may have to come to close the structure. Consider having each of the three outfield positions field and throw simultaneously, as well. An idea may be to have outfielders throw to cutoffs/relays, while others throw to the base. This has purpose because outfielders are coached to throw **through** their relay person. They are not coached to throw **to** them, but rather through them – eye level throws. Infielders can then practice moving their bodies to keep the relay moving to their glove side. Other outfielders can throw all the way through, in a more "do or die" approach.

There are a lot of other resources and books that are designed for full-team drills. Use them!

Have a plan. Have a purpose. Be organized.

COMPETITIVE INDIVIDUAL AND TEAM GAMES

Competitions within practice are healthy and engaging. To keep practice plans from getting stagnant, the following games can be used to build energy, excitement, and competitiveness. Celebrate victories!

Individual Hitting Competition

The scoring system is listed below the chart.

Player Name	Hitters' count	Backside	Hit where it's pitched	0-2 count	Bunting

Notes:

- Each tally is a successful repetition.
- Each player gets five to eight chances. Balls do not count. 0-2 <u>strikes</u> without a swing will result in one negative point.
- Coaches are the judges, and have total say. Complaining or arguments will result in dismissal from entire competition. "Guarantee what you can guarantee."

Scoring:

Hitters count: Ball should be hit hard. Pop ups, swings and misses, foul balls, and weak groundballs are failed attempts. As hitters, we must be aggressive in the "K zone" and attack our hitting strengths.

Backside: Hitters look for pitches they can handle. Balls hit hard up the middle or to the right of the L screen are successful for right-handed hitters. Left-handed hitters must focus at or to the left side of the screen. All others are outs.

Hit it where it's pitched: Watching strikes is a failed attempt in this drill. Balls must be successfully hit with reasonable power based on location—outside, inside pitches. Example: Pulled balls on outer half results in failed attempt. This drill is to promote plate coverage.

0-2: Compete! A successful rep here is contact only because the thrower should be throwing with generally higher velocity and breaking pitches. If the pitch is a strike without a swing, it results in a negative point.

Bunting: Players must successfully bunt the ball to a location determined by coach. Foul balls, misses, and pop ups are all unsuccessful.

Note: This drill is not done with live pitching. This is normal BP pitches.

> *"The most important part of hitting to me is pitch selection. It's important to make decisions about what you're swinging at. We can talk about it all we want, but we must put players in a position to understand pitch selection by physically training for it."*
> *Eddie Smith – Hitting Coach,* Louisiana State University

Whole-Team Hitting Competitions

Incorporating competition is healthy. The following presents three whole-team competitive hitting games. With different versions and variations, decide what's best for your team. You can also add in a defensive aspect in these competitions.

Game #1: Results by Repetition

- Divide the team into two equal groups. One team will hit while the other team is in the field. If there are more than 18 players, extra fielders should be in the outfield; the infield should be positioned appropriately, minus a pitcher.
- One coach pitches, using a screen.
- In a predetermined time (five to eight minutes), each player on the team will rotate through as quickly as possible. Each player gets one *swing*. They do not have to swing at each pitch, and if they take, they get another pitch. Upon hitting the ball, the batter must exit the box immediately for the other player to enter. The team should be lined up near the dugout so that they can rotate quickly.
- After the determined time, the coaches tally the points for the hitting team, using the points' system that follows.
- Switch and repeat, and play as many innings as desired.

Example Points System:
~Swing and miss	-1
~Foul ball	0
~Weak grounder	0
~Pop up	0
~Hard grounder	1
~Deep fly	2
~Base hit	3 (Touches the outfield grass in any way)
~Breaks perimeter	4 (Gets passed the outfielder)
~Homerun	5

Game #2: Three-team Simulated Game:

Instead of playing a full scrimmage, another option is to divide the team into thirds for simulated games. This limits players standing around, and it makes the pace of practice faster and more engaging. Depending on how many players are on the team, the coach will divide the team into three groups, being sure of one pitcher in each group. Two groups remain in the field, while one group hits.

Team A: Five players begin hitting
Team B: Four players play defense, with one player pitching – five total.
Team C: Four players play defense.

This game is played as normal, with three outs. Players or coaches (preferably players) determine who will rest during one of the defensive rotations, as to be sure there are only nine players on the field. One complete inning is after all three teams hit.

For younger ages, or to keep the game moving quickly, coaches can decide to throw with more of a BP look.

Game #3: Ninth Inning - Pressure Situation Game:

This game is a great way to end practice, but beware, it's important to set the stage and expectations prior to implementation. Coaches need to set the standard that complaining about "what's fair" is unacceptable. We want players to compete with determination and confidence in pressure situations. There are nearly unlimited versions of this game; have fun and make it your own!

Divide the team into two groups. One group is of nine positioned players, and the second group of all remaining players will be considered hitters. The coach will present one situation, for just that day – one half inning. A few examples:

- Nobody on, nobody out, defense up one run.
- Bases loaded, two outs. The offense is down one run. Let the defense decide how to play the ball – promote situational play without coach direction. Learn the game!
- Tie game, runner on third, with nobody out! Unfair? No! The pitcher must work to locate good pitches, and the defense is put into a high-pressure situation where they must do all possible to field the ball. The hitters' approach is to look up in the zone.
- Bases loaded, nobody out, defense is up by three runs.
- Bases loaded, nobody out, tie game.

Really, the options are limitless. Allow players to participate in determining factors and appropriate rewards for the winning team. Coaches can also let captains choose – defensive captain and offensive captain. *I do not encourage losing to result in conditioning.* Come up with reasonable ideas for what some will consider unreasonable situations – who cleans the dugout, carries equipment. How the coach presents this game is highly important – energetic and fun! Remember to switch up teams, and when the "impossible" is accomplished, celebrate! A lot! You may want to even consider a home-plate or mound celebration.

TRYOUT FORMAT AND EVALUATION RESOURCES

It is always best practice to be able to evaluate players formally, especially when the team formed includes tryouts and cuts. This helps the coach keep an organized approach in team formation, and it also allows for more productive conversation when speaking with players about their team status. The following pages will provide three examples of evaluation forms that can be modified to match your appropriate team needs.

Every effort should be made to keep tryouts as organized as possible. Coaches should also keep in mind how they're going to evaluate. Just as important as normal practices, limit standing around as much as possible. Most teams are formed through evaluations that are much more than just physical talent. If looking at the whole player, be cognizant of how a player hustles, handles failure, follows simple directions, and interacts with potential teammates.

Rating Scales:

Rating players based on a scale is not an exact science. It is mostly based on the eye test after years of experience seeing large amounts of players with varying athletic abilities. Some coaches use a 1-3 scale. This allows a bit broader range: 1 = poor, 2 = average, 3 = above average. Others use the same type of system, but expand to 1-5. Using a number system can be subjective, however they allow for organized, reflective consideration when evaluating players.

Major League scouts use a 20-80 scale, or sometimes a 2-8. A 20-80 scale allows for intervals of five. This can also be applied for varsity-aged players, seen in one of the evaluation examples. For the purpose of demonstrating this scale, the scouting guidelines follow:

20 – Poor	30 – Well below average	40 – Below average
50 – Major League average	60 – Above average	70 – Exceptional
	80 – Top tier, elite skill	

To put this into further context with easy-to-measure skills, an average fastball with good location would be 93 miles per hour for most MLB teams. If a scout lists a "50 fastball," the player is typically consistent in that range with good command. For speed, a 4.0 seconds home-to-first time is considered to be an elite, "80 runner" from the right side. It should be noted that home-to-first in this context is from contact of the ball off the bat, to first contact made with first base. A "50 runner" runs in 4.3 seconds in baseball.

On the evaluation sheets, simply use running speed time and velocity (if able) instead of a scale. If velocity is unknown, a scale is helpful. Running can simply be home-to-first, home-to-second, or a 60-yard dash.

Making Cuts:

Do them in person! If at all possible, coaches must have the decency to speak with players face-to-face. Posting rosters or lacking personal communication shows disrespect and weakness. If anything, players deserve a phone call. It helps to have evaluations in front of you as you speak. Certainly, players can be given completed evaluation sheets, but it also serves the purpose of keeping conversation direct and to the point. General guidelines:

- Tell the player within the first couple of sentences. There is no reason to build suspense.
- Keep conversation short and precise.
- Thank the player for trying out.
- Be direct and may eye contact.
- Encourage the player to continue working toward their goals, and perhaps consider other options such as recreational leagues.

Tryouts should be no less than two days, and no more than five days in duration. A one-day tryout may work for small numbers, especially if the team has a lot of returning members. But to truly assess a player takes more than a few groundballs and swings. Conversely, extending over five days is unnecessary. Tryouts should be entirely evaluative, with minimal, to no instruction.

Warm Up:

Set aside time for players to not only warm up via stretching and throwing, but allow an opportunity to field groundballs and take swings without being part of the normal evaluation process. This will allow players to get warmed up appropriately and also reduce nervousness.

The following example is based on a two-day tryout, but depending on numbers, this may have to be expanded over more than two days.

Evaluation Examples:

Adjust to fit your needs! The whole-team example is to serve as a preliminary snapshot, similar to what scouts will use to initially identify players. The more in-depth evaluations are for finalization purposes as the team is formed.

Example Tryout Structure and Format

Day 1:
Stretch and throw
Fielding and hitting rotations

Rotation one:

- Outfielders begin hitting in the cages. They may take 15 swings and utilize tee work and side toss. This is non-evaluative.
- Infielders begin with a series of groundballs from their desired position as a warm up.
- Upon the completion of warm-up groundballs, all infielders go to shortstop for a series of groundballs, with throws to first. Catchers can participate or receive balls from first base to feed to the coach. Players rotate after each set rather than fielding all balls at the same time:
  - Two normal groundballs
  - One ball hit deep to their left
  - One ball hit deep to their right
  - One slow roller

Rotation two:

- Infielders rotate to the cages.
- Outfielders begin with a series of flyballs and groundballs as a warm up.
- Upon the completion of warm-ups, all outfielders go to right field. The coach will hit either flyballs or groundballs, and the outfielder throws to each location. Players can rotate to bases to receive throws.
  - Two balls thrown to second base
  - Two balls thrown to first base
  - Two balls thrown home

Full-squad infield/outfield: Players go to their desired position.

- Outfield goes to 2B one time.
- Outfield goes to 3B one time.
- Outfield goes to home two times. Outfield will then remain in position.
- Each infield position fields and throws home one time.

- Each infield position fields and throws to 1B one time.
- Each infield position turns a double play, 2B to 1B, one time.
- Each infield position fields a slow-roller, to be thrown to 1B.
- Pop up communication and priority – the coach will hit a number of flyballs in all areas of the field.

Catcher pop times
Batting practice round. Refer to chapter seven for team hitting structure.
Field clean up.

Day Two:
Stretch and throw.
Full-team diamond drill (Chapter seven).
Outfield goes with a coach for warm-up routine, including groundballs, and flyballs.
Infield circus (Chapter seven) – *one-minute sets only*.
Full-team infield/outfield, repeat from day one or expand repetitions.
Scrimmage.

Scrimmage Ideas:

- The batting orders are full-team. Everyone hits live.
- Use chapter eight to design a three-team scrimmage.
- Organize a scrimmage to have players play specific positions – the coach's discretion – in specific innings, including innings in which the player sits. Each player must preview the chart to know where they're playing in a given inning.
- Allow a sandlot approach. Design a team batting order to be followed and an initial position, but allow players to then rotate to different positions. Mandate that they rotate a certain amount of times. This will show players' willingness to play a position different than where they desire. Pitchers will still be given specific innings to pitch.
- Coaches can coach a base, or watch behind a protective screen directly behind home plate, or in the stands. Playing a sandlot style game allows coaches to see communication, leadership, teammate interaction, adjustments, selflessness/selfishness, and compromise.

Full-Team Evaluation Chart Sample

2 – Poor

3 – Well below average   5 – High school average   7 – Very good

4 – Below average   8 – Division 1 tool

6 – Above average

Name, Position, Year	Bats (L/R)	Throws L/R)	Arm	Field	Hit	Power	Speed	Status Yes/No	GPA

Pitcher Eval

Name	Throw L/R	Fast Ball	FB Control	Breaking Ball	BB Control	Change Up	CH Control	Other	Other Control

Individual Evaluation Chart Sample One

Name:

Year: **Bat/Throw:**   **Position:**   **GPA:**

Tool	Score	Comments
Hit		
Power		
Arm		
Field		
Speed		

Hustle and make up:

Pitchers

Name:

Year: **Throw:**

Pitch	Score/Velo	Comments
Fastball		
Breaking		
Change		
Other		

Arm action and delivery:

Pitching presence:

Individual Evaluation Chart Sample Two

Player Name: _____   **Position:** _____   **Year:** _____

GPA: _____   **Bats/Throws:** _____

Exit Velocity: _____   **Running Speed:** _____

Defensive comments – glove, arm, instincts.

Hitting comments – hitting ability, power potential, plate coverage.

Pitching comments – Velocity, off-speed, command (control), pitching presence.

Player status

Cut	Made

RECRUITING

Film Preparation, Contacts, and College Culture – The Blunt Truth

Coaches of all levels will recruit specifically for their program. One player does not always draw interest from all coaches of the same level. I have heard parents and players with sour grapes express that they do not understand how someone was recruited by a particular coach and not someone else. The answer? The coach saw something they liked. Period.

Body Language is Everything:

This is true for all players and all positions. Baseball and softball are sports of failure. Especially if you know that you're being watched, it can be difficult to accept not being successful in any aspect of the game, but it is extremely difficult when hitting because all eyes are fixed on you. You will not find a college coach that hasn't crossed a potential prospect off of their list for poor behavior during their evaluation. The first time I truly understood this was when my college coach, Coach Burbridge was watching me play for the final time. It was during the travel season following my high school career, and after game one I sat in the stands with Coach to discuss signing. He was watching one of my teammates closely until that player popped up, cursed loudly, threw his bat, and walked down to first base. Coach smiled, we shook hands, and he said he'd see me in a week. Stories like this happen often. I once witnessed a player ridicule his mom for purchasing the wrong colored sports drink! Easy cross off. Coaches will work with young people, and sometimes circumstances don't allow for a young player to understand limits and standards. But generally speaking, coaches will **not** waste time on a player who does not show reasonable maturity and self-control.

> *"Other than obvious talent, I'm looking for what separates players, such as their make up and hustle. College brings a lot more challenges than they're getting in high school and travel, and I want to know how they are as a teammate."*
>
> *Eddie Smith – Hitting Coach*, Louisiana State University

Understand that a "bad day" at the plate will not necessarily discourage coaches from recruiting a player. Do not underestimate their ability to evaluate hitters specifically for their specific recruiting needs. Bad body language, in most cases, will absolutely ruin your chances. This includes cursing, throwing equipment, not running out a fly ball or grounder, and other noticeable gestures. Showing fire and energy is *wanted*, but not poor sportsmanship and pouting. There is a fine line. Excitement, grit, some arrogance, and a tough demeanor are usually preferred. Laziness and lack of class are not.

Parents – this includes you. Screaming at your child (or someone else's), disparaging comments towards coaches and umps, or attempting to coach from the stands are all red flags. Many (most) coaches will walk away from that **quicker than anything else.** You will not find a coach that hasn't moved on from a prospect due to parental behavior. Finally, stay away from the dugout!

Primary Look-For:

In truth, coaches typically do not put much stock into stat lines. Homeruns are great and stand out, but a hitter that doesn't have a particularly good statistical day doesn't *necessarily* mean that they're a bad hitter. Good at-bats can still lead to outs.

Coaches look for production of the swing. A great at-bat can result in an out, but ultimately, the most important thing a coach is looking for is quite simple: Can you hit? College coaches have confidence in themselves as developmental leaders, so a mechanical flaw is not going to deter a coach unless a player simply can't hit. Aggressive, repeated, and controlled barrel contact tells more of the story than mechanics.

> *"I look for how the ball comes off the bat. I feel that pitch selection is a critical piece, as well as what level they compete at within their at-bats. It is great to be able to work with a hitter at a camp or clinic to see how they are able to make adjustments and ultimately evaluate their responses to success and failure. The mental part of hitting is huge, so seeing how they are able to respond to different variables is critical. I like to see if they can stay in the moment and stay locked in on the next repetition or next pitch."*
> *Keith Parr – Head Softball Coach,* Christopher Newport University

Coaches must see an approach. Swinging at pitches out of the zone and being late on fastballs down the heart of the strike zone indicate a lack of fundamental understanding and ability. Regardless of the college level, there is a big jump from high school to college, and the pacing is not always friendly to hitters without an approach.

> *"We want players that produce results. A player's swing can look good but if you cannot consistently barrel the ball, you can't hit."*
> *Joe Abraham – Head Softball Coach,* University of Toledo

Finally, remember that you're not in college yet. Coaches make projections and understand that you're likely to improve significantly from your high school playing days through just the first fall of organized practices. You'll be stronger, more confident, and smarter through the experiences of playing with other collegiate athletes.

Creating Adequate Film:

The truth is, much of the film college coaches receive, even from supposed recruiting services, is inadequate in production. Coaches want to spend no more than three to five minutes watching film, and some will delete the message within seconds. For general film creation, use these guidelines:

- Dress in baseball or softball attire. Look professional.
- Briefly introducing yourself to the camera is fine – name, year, position, high school, travel team.
- Music. Stop. If coaches want music, they'll play their own.
- Video of running speeds, pop times, exit velocities, and pitching speeds that are displayed on screen are ignored. Social media is plastered with false, laughable readings that are mocked in coaching circles. Sometimes those stats aren't even measured correctly – as in how to do it. When a coach determines that they like your film, they'll use proper equipment for measurable tools. Film is not for stats; it's to demonstrate athletic ability and mechanics. As a coach, I have sat at my desk to watch catcher pop times, only to see a very different time flash on the screen than the stop watch I was holding.
- In general, game film is not desired. Coaches want multiple reps in a short amount of time. They will not spend a lot of time watching laborious reps. Pitching is an exception. Coaches would rather see multiple batting practice reps than highlights of successful, in-game swings. They'll will come see you play for those!
- Film is a snapshot, not a life story. Short and sweet is best: 3-5 minutes is plenty.
- Slow motion anything? No.
- Stay away from the dramatics – slow motion, inspirational music. Coaches are looking for athletes to help them win, not a movie trailer. That's wasted time, effort, and **money.**

Unfortunately, some services charge a substantial amount of money to create a video with flare. It's unnecessary and annoying. Coaches are very specific in what they're looking for – grades, athletic ability, and character.

Hitting-Specific Film:

- Angle 1: The recorder is set to the open side of the hitter, so that the coach can watch their front side. This allows the coach to see balance, timing, looseness of the hands, bat path, bat speed and other desired mechanics. Take 8-10 cuts only.
- Angle 2: If in a cage or on the field, behind the batter. This will show the flight of the ball because a swing can look good but not produce. This will show a slight demonstration of power and ability to hit to all parts of the field.

Appropriate Emails to College Coaches

On any given day, college coaches receive potentially dozens of emails from student athletes. Keep emails short, sweet, and to the point. I encourage parents and players with college desires to consider the following precise and highly important points:

- The player must email the coach, *not the parent*! An initial parent email is immediately deleted by most. Coaches want young, mature adults, not pampered children. The parents will be part of the recruiting process, but they're *not a kid's agent*.

- Edit for reasonable grammar. Coaches are not looking to edit term papers, but a lack of basic writing conventions shows carelessness and a lack of attention to detail. Capital letters and punctuation is, at minimum, expected from a high school athlete.
- Direct it to the specific coach you're contacting! "Coach" is too vague. Coaches understand that you're likely sending the exact same email to a number of coaches, especially if it's through particular recruiting services, or leading up to a showcase event. Make sure you're sending it to the right coach, as well! Coaches have received emails with the wrong name titled. Ouch.
- Stay away from clichés. "It's my dream to play for…" This reads as begging.
- Articles and newspaper clippings are for your parents' scrapbook, not the coach.
- What does "your program" even mean? Like as addressing the correct coach, saying "your program" without actually knowing anything about the program is also careless, or a sign of blast emails.
- If you want to actually play college athletics, take the time to look into their college. Seek majors and other desires that are important for the decision. If you're emailing a coach because you're going to a major showcase event, it's perfectly acceptable to drop a short email and explain that you are interested in meeting and would like to hear more about their program. Being too vague, which really is to also be a phony, is a turn off to coaches.
- If you have *accurate* readings that are confirmed, listing measurable numbers is ok but they must be honest!

"Coaches are often reading emails from their phone, so consider how long it may appear on a small screen. Put video at the top of the page. Some coaches may click on your link before even reading the email!"

Chris Siedem – Perfect College Match, LLC

Sample Email:

Subject Line: Name, Position, Year
<Video link>

Coach Smith:

My name is Jane Doe, and I am currently a junior at John Doe High School in Smith City, Michigan. I am interested in speaking with you to learn more about the softball program at Humphrey University. I am interested in entering the Education Department, as my goal is to be an elementary teacher. My current overall GPA is 3.87

I am the catcher and team captain for my high school team, and I also play for the Travelers during my travel ball season. My schedule is attached, and I will be attending your showcase camp in July.

I look forward to hearing from you and discussing Humphrey University more!

Sincerely,
Jane Doe
High School Coach: Name and number
Travel Ball Coach: Name and number

Above All, Grades Matter Most
And Watch Your Social Media Behavior

Playing College Athletics isn't Easy – at Any Level:

Of my high school teammates, 12 played college baseball. Three of us played for four years. Some didn't make it beyond the fall. Playing college athletics is difficult and it poses challenges that some players have never seen. In an era of "elite" everything, some players move on to the college level with very little understanding and grasp of being coached a little harder, having to earn every role, and playing for **team wins**. While individual success is still great, and there is nothing wrong with feeling good about yourself, it is now **solely about the team** when you get to the college level.

> *"Incoming freshman need to understand overall accountability. They are now on their own, in a new situation. They must step up maturity level and search for solutions to make things happen for themselves."*
> *Keith Parr – Head Softball Coach,* Christopher Newport University

Perhaps one of the biggest false narratives is that lower college levels are a mere extension of high school. This could not be further from the truth. Regardless of the collegiate level, athletes are tasked with balancing a schedule that likely includes early-morning lifting/conditioning sessions, daily and varying class schedules, further practice time, and possibly mandatory study hall – along with expected self-training time. Loving a sport is not enough. Wanting to play in college is not enough. It can't be just a simple idea – "I want to play college ball." It is about commitment, team-first attitude, putting feelings aside, and playing with an effort and intensity that likely hasn't been emphasized **for a sustained period of time**.

> *"I think one of the biggest issues incoming players must adjust to is that everything we do is built around winning; it's not about personal stats and playing time anymore. They also have to learn that winning over a four-game weekend tournament is not real winning. It is about the process of a long, grueling season of ups and downs."*
> *Bill Cilento – Associate Head Baseball Coach,* Wake Forest University

College sports are hard. For freshman, the learning curve is often eye-opening and underestimated. Some players decide after one year that the commitment simply "isn't worth it." Some leave during the season. Some leave after fall practice. I have even coached a player that endured *one* morning of conditioning and quit.

But the commitment *is* worth it. Whether you're a player on a large scholarship or playing with no athletic financial support, good teams are good teams and the life-long take-aways are invaluable.

Friendships are life-long: I know I speak for the large majority in saying that the first thought that comes to our mind is the bond and friendships formed. Teammates form a brotherhood or sisterhood, and while some friendships remain strong for life, even those players who drift away over time carry the bloodlines of the college institution, engrained forever. The hugs, tears, and heartbreak when seasons finally end are more about saying goodbye to your brothers and sisters than it is the pain of the loss or ended season. In baseball and softball, you can keep playing recreational leagues so long as your body can handle it, but you will never get those times back, on and off the field. I conducted a social media poll and 99% of the responses said their fondest memories are about the bonds they formed. There is really no way to understand it without experiencing it.

Life-long lessons: Great coaches are usually seen as such based on wins and losses, but the best of the best leave the deepest impact, sometimes deeper than some young athletes receive from home. Coaches should challenge players physically and mentally, and this is part of the life-long equation. There simply aren't enough pages I could write to explain the impact Coach Hank Burbridge had on my life. Good coaches do not only improve your physical ability. **They improve your *life*.**

Marketable: I don't know if playing college athletics had anything to do with being hired in various teaching positions. But there is a lot to be said for former athletes in terms of their ability to handle adversity with relative calmness, receive critical feedback without being too sensitive, and to see a big-picture approach. All can be correlated to the types of conditions players endure over a four-year (or more) playing career. Each of the areas are completely related to playing athletics. It is said that young people that participate in team activities/athletics are more well-rounded. So are adults.

Oh, it's worth it.

PRIVATE HITTING INSTRUCTORS

Weighing the Good and the Bad

There are "hitting instructors" all over country. Some are outstanding, teaching with a high level of knowledge and understanding, and some that have no business working with young people. This is a "touchy" subject of sorts because you're dealing with what could be someone's primary source of income. Precisely because they're working with your son or daughter, it's ok and important to ask questions, however!

Do Your Research and Ask Questions:

Speaking with other parents could be a catch-22. Everyone has different experiences, and in the sports' world, one bruised ego could be a determining factor for a "bad coach." If you're contemplating working with a coach, instead of relying on feedback from others, go directly to the coach. Request to watch him or her working with an athlete, or ask specific questions regarding their developmental approach. Center your questions around the coach's philosophies and ideals, their developmental approach, and goal-setting. How will progress be measured? What does a progression plan look like?

Good Hitting Instructors' Commonalities:

- Good coaches evaluate before teaching. A coach that begins with a mechanical focus early on should be alarming. The first time with a player should be almost entirely evaluative. Remember that less is more. A good hitting coach may put a hitter through a series of drills, including tee work, side toss, and normal front toss.
- Good coaches diagnose a swing, **then develop a proper plan**. Diagnosing is easy. The solution is not always as easy. What are they going to do to allow the hitter to improve?
- Good coaches have clear expectations, and they are different from player-to-player.
- Good coaches can rationalize *everything* they're doing, from drills to adjustments made in swings. They should be able to explain in full, with examples and concrete, jargon-free rationale.
- Good coaches may use words like launch angle, rotational, and linear, but they're not focused on it. Jargon words oftentimes sell because parents hear them from others so assume that it demonstrates knowledge.

- Good coaches engage with their players and develop basic relationships.
- Good coaches know the whole hitter – mechanics and approach. Watch for coaches that zero in on one particular concept and continue to hammer it. There should be repeat instruction because we're developing repeat mechanics. But, for example, if a coach is exhausting one aspect of hitting, seemingly irrelevant, it is probably because they once heard an instructor use the same verbiage, therefore they run with someone else's ideas, and lack ability to expand.
- Good coaches use video with a purpose. Video could be that of the student's swing, or demonstration of high-level hitters. Video is not used to create a swing model; it's used instead to help the player understand their own mechanics and to be cognizant of self.
- Good coaches get off their butt! Some drills are done with a seated thrower. But laziness should be avoided. Coaches shouldn't plant themselves on a chair for 45 minutes.
- Good coaches do not rely on a pitching machine. Pitching machines are good for some drills, but overall, good hitting instructors use them minimally.
- Good coaches work together with travel and high school coaches, not against. This is uncommon because one of the coaches is often reluctant to learn from someone else or put forth the effort for the athlete.

Private instructor red flags:

- Promises. Promising equates to begging. It's perfectly acceptable for a coach to sell themselves, but be careful of empty promises such as getting players into particular colleges, or guarantees of throwing velocities, exit velocities, and the like. "If you come to me, I guarantee you'll be throwing 70 miles per hour in just three months." You cannot possibly *guarantee* that with honesty. Coaches should instead set *realistic goals* and **develop an achievement plan.** The best coaches put responsibility on the player because ultimately, the success is in the player's work.
- Too much jargon. Catch words and jargon should also include substance and rationale.
- Degrading comments toward other coaches. This can be difficult because if a coach is working with a player that has quite obviously been taught incorrect fundamentals, changes may be necessary. It will be up to the coach to not jump to conclusions, hear the player and parents out, and then decide a plan of action. A more tactful way to approach an athlete that has been clearly misinformed is to simply focus on what they're doing, not what someone else did. Immediately degrading a previous coach is a sign of weakness.
- Every player does the exact same thing, including drills and mechanics. The most effective drills are often the ones used the most. If they work, use them! But if *every* lesson looks the same, it shows a lack of understanding of the individual.

- Hard promotion of former athletes in college. Athletes are most responsible for their success. Instructors enjoy the success of their athletes, and there is nothing wrong with sharing that success. But there is a fine line in sharing and simply taking credit for the success. Boasting about a player going to an elite school is quite different than applauding the young person's accomplishments. The best instructors seem to distance themselves from self-promotion through a student athlete.
- Liars and fakes. This point is last because it's the most sensitive. It is also the most compromising for young people. Lying comes in many sad forms, and one of the worst is **knowingly and falsely branding kids' skillsets for all the world to see**. Eventually those numbers and misleading information will catch up, and families are left with finger-pointing options. This is a problem, especially on social media, and its impact is on **the child athlete.**

Do these private lessons help? Is there improvement? Are they measurable? Are the coaches simply dishing out false praise to keep you coming back? Parents and players cannot expect magic and instant success. That is, in fact, a problem in our athletic society today. We want immediate success but that is rarely possible. Hold players accountable for their own learning and their work after lessons, even at young ages. The work done *after* lessons and clinics is as important – if not more – than the lesson itself. A "lesson" is to educate. Good coaches and teachers educate, not simply instruct. Expect the player to be able to explain what they have done at lessons, even if it's minimal in response.

> *"Private instructors can feel obligated to fix something, or talk after every pitch, usually with a parent hovering over the batting cage. More often than not, the only thing really needed is a quality round of batting practice."*
> Keith Werman – Development Coordinator, San Diego Padres

Amen to this. The fact is, as previously stated, less talk is usually more effective. Do not expect constant verbal feedback. Expect lessons with purpose and growth.

EPILOGUE

Bring Back Play

It's difficult to write a book on hitting that includes all credited sources without also crediting a powerful component of hitting development that is all but lost in playgrounds and yards across America.

Nobody plays anymore.

Kids practice and participate in games and tournaments, sometimes in highly excessive amounts. Indoor games starting in January. Fall seasons ending in late November. Sometimes there is no rest period, which by the way is absolutely condoned by every credible source in the coaching world.

As a teacher of elementary students for many years, it's evident that kids simply do not **play** as much as previous generations. Everything is scripted. There is a coach or private instructor always engaged. As a result, our youth is losing the ability to problem solve, and even worse, lack the time to simply play with peers in an unorganized setting. I have had many conversations about this issue, so I feel as someone promoting good hitting instruction, I would be bordering neglect if I didn't at least offer up advice in the area of playing.

Just playing. With friends. No coaches.

When I was growing up in Northern Michigan, my best friend and I developed a game that would work with limited players, even if it was just one-on-one. During those years, before I played travel ball around ninth grade, we only played roughly twenty games during the summer. Mention that today and it's almost unfathomable. Twenty games! Some kids now are playing over twenty games in one *month*. Even though we didn't play excessive amounts of games, I am absolutely certain that I had as many at-bats during the summer months as our youth softball and baseball players are getting today. They were purposeful at-bats, too! We switch hit, and we learned to compete as a hitter. And sometimes it was just two of us, in the front yard, playing for hours. The experience of simply playing with friends is easily the most beneficial hitting development I had during my youth.

Video games. Private coaches. Travel Coaches. Analytical breakdown. Technology in swings. I'm not sure if we'll ever again see an America with kids simply playing baseball in their yards, but there is a simple way to enjoy the game. If anything, it's necessary because verbal communication in our youth is severely lacking, and its decline is not only significant, but definitive.

Play. Please.

Front Yard Baseball:

Sta's and I created a game in his front yard that was anything but Earth shattering, yet kept us playing hard throughout the beautiful Northern Michigan summer months. His stepdad put four-by-fours together to create a square backstop. The screening was made of a heavy, black plastic, and the strike zone was painted on.

Some days we had several friends join us, but most often is was just Sta's and I. We used a ragball and stood at roughly Little League distance to pitch, making the velocity a bit more difficult, and with a ragball, we were able to manipulate its movement. Sometimes we simply played as we were, but because of TV coverage, our line-ups matched the Atlanta Braves, Detroit Tigers, and Chicago Cubs. We hit like each hitter, from their particular side of the plate, to their individual stance. Cecil Fielder's hitch. Tony Philips' low crouch. Terry Pendelton's ultra-open stance. Mickey Tettleton's unorthodox pre-pitch look.

The rules were quite simple, whether one-on-one or multiple players. There was no base running. Lazy fly balls in the field of play were automatic outs. If the ball was hit, the defense had until "four one-thousand" to retrieve the ball and throw it at the mat. If they did so before "four one-thousand" it was considered an out. If there was a double play situation and the ball hit the strike zone, it was considered a double play, to be determined by the defense. In such cases, if the bases were loaded with no outs, a double play would have been considered home-to-first. If the hitter decided to advance to second base, they had to get to "eight one-thousand" before the defense hit the mat, and so on, through "twelve one-thousand" for a triple. If the defense hit the mat, they were thrown out; there was no returning to the base. We had "fences," appropriately dimensional for centerfield and the corners.

Yes, there would be a lot of running because if the ball was not hit directly at the pitcher, you had to sprint to retrieve it, especially if either you thought you could hit the mat by four-one-thousand or if they were going to attempt a double. And that's ok!

Kids need to play. They need to play for not only fun and physical activity, but also for social development, problem solving, and compromise. Going to a quality hitting instructor and playing quality travel ball is part of the landscape, and that's not changing. It's a multi-*billion* dollar industry.

But playing is priceless.

Special thanks to Sta's Rozanski for your support and friendship, and the persuasive ability to get me to throw 80 pitches in your front yard prior to an evening game. In all of my athletic memories, those days in the front yard are at the top.

CREDITS AND CONTRIBUTIONS

Gratitude for the individuals that helped support this book through conversation and design cannot be expressed enough. Hank Burbridge always emphasized surrounding yourself with good people. I have done so, and as a result, it has helped me grow tremendously as a coach, instructor, and leader of youth.

- **Jim Thompson:** Mid-Atlantic Area Supervisor for the New York Mets.
- **Keith Werman:** Former four-year starter at the University of Virginia and now works with the San Diego Padres as the Development Coordinator, with focus on infielders and hitters.
- **Derrick May:** Played ten years in the Major Leagues and is a highly regarded hitting instructor. During his Major League tenure, Coach May spent time with the Cubs, Brewers, Astros, Phillies, Expos and Orioles. In addition to his playing career, he has experience coaching at both the Major League and Minor League levels.
- **Eddie Smith:** Hitting Coach at Louisiana State University. Coach Smith has been an assistant at University of Virginia, University of Notre Dame, Santa Clara University, and Tulane University. He was also the head coach at Lower Columbia College for four years.
- **Bill Cilento:** Regarded as one of the top offensive minds in Division I college baseball. He serves as Associate Head Coach and Hitting Coach at Wake Forest University.
- **Joe Abraham:** Head Softball Coach at the University of Toledo. Coach Abraham also served as Head Softball Coach at NCAA Division II Hillsdale College for seven years.
- **Jake Boss:** Head Baseball Coach at Michigan State University and previous head coach at Eastern Michigan University.
- **Keith Parr:** Head Softball coach at NCAA Division III power, Christopher Newport University, located in Newport News, Virginia.
- **Andy Pascoe:** Assistant Baseball Coach and Recruiting Coordinator at Butler University. Coach Pascoe began his coaching career at his alma mater, University of Evansville.
- **Tom Compian:** Assistant Coach at Lawrence Tech University in the greater Detroit, Michigan area, working with outfielders and base runners. Coach Humphrey's Spring Arbor University teammate.
- **Ricky Gregg:** Outstanding private hitting instructor, coach, and owner of the Yard Baseball and Softball academy in Roanoke, Virginia.
- **Chris Siedem:** Owner of Perfect College Match and works with players throughout the country on an intimate basis, helping athletes find fits to compete at the college level.

- **Logan Mann:** Head Baseball coach at NCAA Division III Lakeland College, in Wisconsin and spent ten years at Southern Virginia University as the head coach.
- **George Lasse:** Long-time Valley Baseball League coach and manager, as well as the head coach at Staunton High School, in Virginia.
- **Linda McGinnis:** Years of head coaching experience, current co-owner of Turn 2 Sports, and head softball coach of Turn 2 Softball, based out of the greater Baltimore, Maryland area.

Book Support:
- Many thanks to Jeff Burton, General Manager of the Charlottesville Tom Sox, of the Valley Baseball League. Jeff, a former University of Virginia player and area youth coach, was instrumental in supporting this book, from facility use to a liaison in working with various coaches.

Photos
- Interior Photos by James Beeler
- Cover Design by Bobby Humphrey and Kendra Nicholson

Editing
- Thanks to my former student, Emilia Munro, for suggesting her mother, Julia Munro PhD, for editing.
- Justin Beard, a personal friend.

Bat Supplier
- Odie bats, by Scott Edwards. Scott is a former teammate at Spring Arbor University and creates specialized bats for coaches and players of all ages.

Book Title Creation
- Special thanks to Elseay Bousquet, who came up with the idea for the title of this book. Elseay was a fifth-grade student in Coach Humphrey's class during the 2018-2019 school year.

ABOUT THE AUTHOR

Bobby Humphrey originally hails from Traverse City, Michigan and enjoyed a blessed playing career that included playing under some exceptional coaches and leaders. At Traverse City Central High School, Humphrey was coached by one of Michigan's most well-respected high school coaches, Ian Hearn. While at Spring Arbor University, he had the unique privilege to play for two thousand-game winners and Hall of Famers, Hank Burbridge and Sam Riggleman.

Coach Humphrey's coaching career includes experience with all ages, youth through the college level on both the baseball and softball fields. Coach Humphrey has had stints at the varsity level as assistant and head coach, as well as multiple years as an assistant college coach. He has worked with thousands of players throughout the country, attending showcases, clinics, and camps.

In addition to his coaching duties, Coach Humphrey began as an Associate Scout with the New York Mets in 2009, supporting the mid-Atlantic region, as well as the Valley Baseball League. During his scouting career, he has evaluated hundreds of drafted prospects from all rounds of the MLB draft. His experience as an evaluator has helped tremendously in development of hitters. He published his first book, *The Tools of Greatness*, in 2013 and its second edition in 2015.

Humphrey currently lives in Virginia, with his wonderful wife, Kendra, and teaches in the public school system.